BK 629.229 S524C
COMPLETE BOOK OF ELECTRIC VEHICLES
/SHACKET, S
C1979 14.50 FV

3000 553920 30012
St. Louis Community College

W9-DIM-995

WITHDRAWN

629.229 S524c   FV
SHACKET
THE COMPLETE BOOK OF ELECTRIC
VEHICLES
                              14.50

St. Louis Community
College

Library

5801 Wilson Avenue
St. Louis, Missouri 63110

the Complete Book of
ELECTRIC VEHICLES

by Sheldon R. Shacket

DOMUS BOOKS
Chicago • New York

LIBRARY
ST. LOUIS COMMUNITY COLLEGE
AT FLORISSANT VALLEY

BOOK DESIGN AND PRODUCTION: **MacDonald-Ball Studio**
EDITORIAL DIRECTOR: **Betty Ritter**
SPECIAL ILLUSTRATIONS: **Robert Tanaka**

Copyright © 1979 Quality Books, Inc.
Published by
Domus Books
400 Anthony Trail
Northbrook, Illinois 60062

All rights reserved. Neither the whole nor part of this publication may be reproduced, stored in a retrieval system, or transmitted, in any form or by any means, electronic, mechanical, photocopying, recording, or otherwise, without the prior written permission from Quality Books, Inc., 400 Anthony Trail, Northbrook, Illinois 60062.

Manufactured in the United States of America

3   4   5   6   7   8   9   10

Library of Congress Cataloging in Publication Data

Shacket, Sheldon R. 1941—
The complete book of electric vehicles.

Includes index.
1. Electric vehicles.   I. Title.   II. Title:
Electric vehicles.
TL220.S53   629.22'93   78-12613
ISBN 0–89196–019–8 (paper)
ISBN 0–89196–033–3 (cloth)

Contents

Preface

In October, 1978, I had the privilege of attending the Fifth International Vehicle Symposium in Philadelphia, Pennsylvania. During the Symposium, speakers from all over the world discussed the development of Electric Vehicles. This event was sponsored by the Electric Vehicle Council (EVC), a non-profit organization, and The International Union of Producers and Distributors of Electric Energy (UNIPEDE).

Concurrently, across town, an Electric Vehicle Exposition was held at the Philadelphia Civic Center. Over 25 organizations displayed more than 65 vehicles of all sizes and shapes. Included were electric and electric/hybrid personal cars, vans, buses, trucks, orthopedic equipment, motorcycles, bicycles and industrial carriers. During the four day Exposition, thousands of spectators previewed the very latest technology in batteries, vehicles and components from all over the world.

To keynote the opening of the Expo, an Electric Vehicle parade travelled silently through downtown Philadelphia, from the Franklin Institute to the Civic Center, and Pennsylvania Governor Shapp designated October 1-7 as Electric and Hybrid Vehicle Week.

Later, I reflected upon what I had observed and synthesized the whole experience into one thought: *the Electric Vehicle is coming!* It is an integral part of man's future and survival on this planet. There is no power on earth that can stop this eventual development.

Today we are observing the stepping stones which will bring technology and imagination together to create truly efficient vehicles and energy systems worthy of the 21st Century.

Some day our cities will be powered by the energy of the universe: nuclear fusion. Handfuls of sea water will yield more energy than an oil supertanker. Solar and geothermal systems, wind and wave action, nuclear breeder reactors, microwave energy transmission, waste recycling, and magnetohydrodynamics will combine to produce an electric society. This new society will control its environment to benefit nature, not destroy it. With a little patience, we will see new technological advances emerge like mushrooms in a field. The threshold of a new age is upon us. It is ours to behold.

This book was written for everyone. It is not a scientific dissertation to be filed away in an engineering library. It is a look at what has preceded us, what is now the state of the art, and what the future will hopefully bring. There are no formulas or equations. Explanations are simplified so people of all backgrounds can learn about electric vehicles without being intimidated by technical data. Whenever used, industry jargon and technical terms are explained in simple terms.

As a result, this book may have the effect of persuading the potential electric vehicle enthusiast to research the subject in greater depth. And, hopefully, may also convince a few skeptics. However, if I can help the reader accept the fact that some day the electric vehicle will be commonplace in world transportation, then I will have accomplished my objective.

Sheldon R. Shacket

Introduction

We all remember the gasoline shortages which produced long lines of automobiles waiting at gasoline pumps. Perhaps this was indicative of American overreaction. But whether real or imagined, the 1973-1974 oil crisis has inflated the price of gasoline from 37¢ to over $1.00 a gallon. The days of U.S. oil production supremacy are over. By 1975, our consumption rate made us the second largest importer of oil in the world. A fifty billion dollar annual trade deficit as a result of oil importation is the fruit which our folly has produced.

In this book, we will see that our battery production capabilities of today are adequate to meet demands in the foreseeable future. Also, we will see that the electricity required for electric vehicles in the immediate future will not pose any serious problems because the vehicles can recharge during the evening hours, taking advantage of the excess capacity of conventional and nuclear power stations. In some cases, this is otherwise lost or wasted energy. Finally, because the new electrical demand will not increase the personnel and equipment needs of power stations, we will not have cause for alarm if large numbers of electric vehicles are produced.

Because petroleum is an irreplaceable commodity, we will look at how we can save this natural resource for better and more strategic uses such as air defense, the production of plastics, and the manufacture of fertilizers for agriculture. We will show how the electric vehicle fits into an electric society where the accumulated alternate energy sources will, if intelligently promoted and developed, bring us energy independence.

Today, only 16% of our electricity is generated by petroleum. Coal, hydroelectric, and nuclear energy supply the bulk of our electricity. Therefore, the more vehicles powered by electricity, the less dependent we become on oil for transportation. And because it is easier to control one large power station's emission, using carefully monitored equipment, than it is to maintain internal combustion engines that are never properly "tuned," we will be in a better position to reduce pollution.

Out of the nation's energy crisis and air pollution problems has come a mandate for electric vehicle development. The fact that 87% of all automobile trips are 15 miles or less one way, that on the average our vehicles travel about

10,000 miles per year, that 18,500,000 barrels of oil and 55% of all gasoline in the United States is consumed on our city streets, and that our oil reserves will last between 12 and 25 years in the U.S., underscore the need for electric vehicles.

When we realize that transportation uses about 50% of the petroleum in the U.S., and that virtually all urban pollution is due to the internal combustion engine, the need for electric vehicles becomes clear. We see before us a new and potent industry that will offer overwhelming opportunities. Public need is the handmaiden of all successful business—companies that satisfy the need for electric vehicles will surpass those companies that continue to feed the appetite of the internal combustion engine.

Congressman Mike McCormack, during a recent international electric vehicle exposition in Chicago, said, "There are approximately one hundred million cars in this country; about 40% of these are "second cars." Ninety percent of the second car fleet is replaced approximately every five years. (These are the older cars and many of them are gas guzzlers.) If we can make electric vehicles attractive, safe, and generally competitive with the second cars for the purpose for which they are used, I believe we can have ten million electric vehicles on our streets by 1990, and several tens of millions before the end of the century. This is our goal and your challenge."

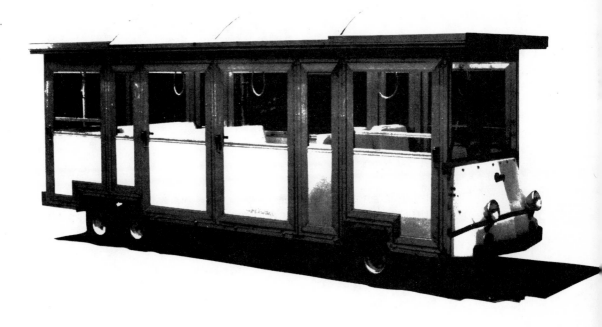

This book is dedicated to Evelyn and Jan Shacket
with many thanks to:
Joseph Seliber, P.E.
William E. Siegfriedt, M.E.
Robert Myers (Know-It-All)
Denise Reig, Arlene Pabian, Nancy Hoffmann,
Phyllis Betenia and John Newell.

chapter 1

Electric Vehicle History

The last decade of the 19th century provided an atmosphere that was particularly suited to the development of new modes of transportation.

The emerging cities required alternatives to the noisy and dirty steam- powered locomotives and horse-drawn city carriages. This was a period when Americans owned over 25 million horses and the principal form of personal transportation was that mechanical marvel, the safety bicycle. Ten million bicycles gave Americans a new freedom—the freedom from feeding and maintaining a horse. The bicycle also encouraged the construction of paved streets and brought about improvements in metallurgy, bearings, wheels, and power transmissions. These technical advances opened the door to a host of mechanized forms of transportation. Suddenly, curious new self-powered vehicles began appearing on city streets. Steam, internal combustion and electric carriages could perform the functions of the horse or bicycle.

The electric vehicle quickly became popular with city dwellers. People had grown familiar with electric trolleys and railways, and technology had produced motors and batteries in a wide variety of sizes. The Edison cell, a nickel-

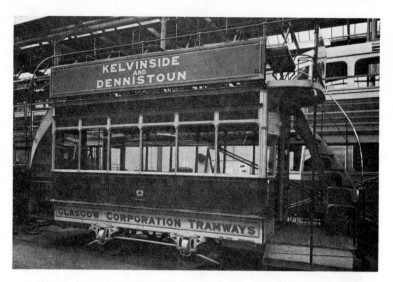

The horse-drawn tramcars of 1894 were converted to electric power after 1898 by the Glasgow, Scotland Department of Transportation. The cars seated 18 passengers inside and 26 outside.

Photo courtesy of
The Museum of Transport, Glasgow

THE CHICAGO INTERMURAL
The world's first electrically operated elevated railroad cars were on display at the World's Columbian Exposition in 1893.

Photo courtesy of
The Chicago Historical Society

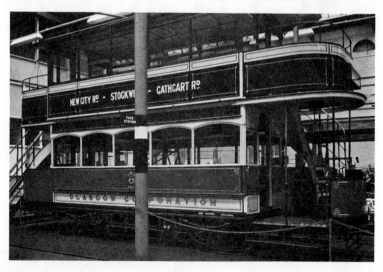

The Standard electric Tram No. 779 of 1900 seated 24 people on the lower level, 42 on top. Scotland Department of Transportation.

Photo courtesy of
The Museum of Transport, Glasgow

iron battery, developed by Thomas Edison in 1910, became the leader in electric vehicle use.

For a short period of time in the early days of automotive development the electric vehicle reigned supreme, and became a dominant factor in the personal transportation scene prior to the turn of the century.

A SIMPLIFIED HISTORY OF EARLY POWERED TRANSPORTATION

This chart depicts the development of various modes of transportation and their relationship to the electric vehicle prior to the turn of the century.

1600	*Simon Steven* of Holland: a wind powered sailing chariot.
1769	*Nicolas Cugnot* of France: a three-wheeled, 3-mph (4.8 km/hr) steam-powered, cannon wagon.
1801	*Richard Trevithick*, England: steam-powered carriage.
1804	*Oliver Evans*, America: steam amphibian.
1822	*Sir Goldworthy Gurney*, England: 30-mph (48 km/hr) steam carriage.
1834	*Thomas Davenport*, America: battery-powered electric car used on a short track (non-rechargeable).
1838	*Robert Davidson*, Scotland: 5-ton electric locomotive (non-rechargeable).
1847	*Moses Farmer*, America: electric car, 2-passenger, non-rechargeable (experimental).
1851	*Charles B. Page*, America: 19-mph (31 km/hr) electric car (non-rechargeable).
1859	*Gaston Plante,*: development of lead storage battery.
1874	*Sir David Salomons*, England: battery-powered carriage.
1879	First non-battery locomotive exhibited in Berlin, Germany.
1881	*Camille Favre,*: storage battery improvement.
1881	First use of a third rail for rail locomotives. (Electricity produced by dynamo generation early in 1870's.)
1885	*Karl Benz*, Germany: gasoline-powered tricycle car.
1886	*Frank J. Sprague:* first successful electric trolley system. (Prior method was horse-drawn rail carriages.)
1886	*Gottlieb Daimler*, Germany: gasoline-powered automobile.
1888	*Fred Kimball*, America: electric car operated in Boston.
1891	*William Morrison*, America: electric car operated in Chicago.
1893	Electric carriages used at Chicago World's Fair to carry visitors.
1893	*Duryea Bros.*, America: gasoline-powered buggy.
1895	First electric rapid transit, Chicago.

Columbia

MARK XI OPERA BUS

For six years Columbia Automobiles have led the motor vehicle procession. Perfection of parts under the most rigorous inspections and tests makes each Columbia Automobile a unit of strength in mechanical construction, art in carriage construction, safety in service, simplicity in operation, reliability in control, ease in riding, and cleanliness in handling. For pleasure touring, transportation and delivery service, there are many standard types to select from. Special bodies can be equipped and long-distance batteries furnished at short notice. Where charging facilities are not convenient, we are prepared to furnish estimates for, and erect when desired, automatic plants for charging electric vehicles. Write for catalogue, or call at any of the following agencies:

STATE OF NEW YORK: New York Electric Vehicle Transportation Co., Sales and Show Rooms, 541 Fifth Ave , New York City.
STATE OF PENNSYLVANIA: Pennsylvania Electric Vehicle Co., 250-256 N. Broad St.. Phila.
STATE OF ILLINOIS: Illinois Electric Vehicle Transportation Co., 173 Michigan Ave., Chicago.
NEW ENGLAND STATES: New England Electric Vehicle Transportation Co., 541 Tremont St., Boston, Mass.
DISTRICT OF COLUMBIA: Washington Electric Vehicle Transportation Co., Panorama Building, Fifteenth St. and Ohio Ave., Washington, D. C.
STATE OF NEW JERSEY: New Jersey Electric Vehicle Transportation Co., 100 Broadway, New York City.
CALIFORNIA OFFICE: Parrott Building, Market Street, San Francisco, Cal.
EUROPEAN OFFICE: 54 Avenue Montaigne, Paris, France.
MEXICO: Mexican Electric Vehicle Co., Primera Humboldt No. 12, Mexico City, Mexico.

In territory not represented by local companies and agencies, all communications should be addressed to

ELECTRIC VEHICLE COMPANY
HARTFORD, CONN. ❧ 100 BROADWAY, N. Y.

1899 RIKER

Photo courtesy of Smithsonian Institute

The turn of the century marked the beginning of electric vehicle dominance in the pleasure car field. In the year 1900, 4,200 automobiles were sold. Of these, 38% were electric, 22% gasoline-powered, and 40% steam.

In the early 1900's, the electric Brougham and Victoria carriages were the preferred method of transportation among New York's wealthy elite. Closed-body electrics followed regal carriage lines many years before gasoline automobiles offered enclosed bodies. Equipped with chauffeur and footmen, the elegant "electrics" carried wealthy families to plays, operas, and fashionable gatherings. Their cost was in the $5,000 to $6,000 range, easily equivalent to a Rolls Royce of today.

Sales of the automobile had risen sharply. Only fifteen years had passed since the development and introduction of the 1885 Karl Benz gasoline-powered tricycle, which used a 110-pound (50 kg), 1/2-horsepower engine. The vehicle could maintain speeds of only a few miles per hour and was unable to negotiate even the mildest grade.

The first primitive American gasoline-powered buggy was the 1893 Duryea. In the same year, electric carriages were already "for hire" at the Chicago World's Fair. Early development and expert marketing gave electrics a clear edge over gasoline-powered vehicles.

In this period, the bicycle industry in America was very strong. The largest bicycle maker in America was the Pope Manufacturing Company. Pope "Columbia" bicycles were respected throughout the world. But Colonel Albert A. Pope, the company's founder, believed that, although the bicycle was the simplest form of transportation imaginable, requiring little care, producing no pollution, and providing healthful exercise for the owner, there was a clear cut destiny for the electric car and truck. By the end of 1898, Pope had produced about 500 electric automobiles under the name ''Columbia Electric.''

In 1899, the Pope firm was purchased by the Electric Vehicle Company. The EVC was a huge conglomerate by the standards of that day and pursued the acquisition of all electric car and taxi companies in the United States. Its net worth was over 18 million dollars in 1899, yet by 1907, having staked everything on the continuing dominance of electrics over gasoline-powered vehicles, it was totally bankrupt.

Another early electric car manufacturer was the Electric Carriage and Wagon Company owned by Henry G. Morris and Pedro G. Salom. The Morris and Salom ''Electrobat'' cab of 1895-1897 operated in New York City in January 1897 in a fleet of twelve public taxis. Like Pope, the company was absorbed by The Electric Vehicle Company.

The Riker Electric Motor Company of America was founded by A. L. Riker in 1896 and produced a variety of electric cars and trucks until

1904 COLUMBIA
Photo courtesy of
the Smithsonian Institute

1914 RAUCH & LANG

Photo courtesy of the Smithsonian Institute

1902. After Riker sold out to the Electric Vehicle Company, he began producing gasoline vehicles.

The Krieger Company of Paris, France, was an important contributor to electric vehicle technology and was awarded a prize at the 1897 Paris Motor Cab Trials. This amazing vehicle had four-wheel brakes and power steering utilizing a motor on each of the front wheels. The speed of 15 mph (24 km/hr) and range of 50 miles (80 km) per charge was respectable for the 2,530-pound (1147 kg) carriage. M. Krieger was an ingenious man who experimented with an alcohol-electric hybrid in 1902. In 1904, he marketed, without much success, a car powered by both gasoline and electricity. Before his company went into bankruptcy, he patented a turbine-electric hybrid. Fairly advanced for 1909!

The French B.G.S. Electric Car of 1900 held the world's electric distance record of almost 180 miles per charge (290 km). The B.G.S. company made cars, trucks, buses, and limousines from 1899 to 1906. They designed and produced batteries specifically for their own vehicles.

The Woods Motor Vehicle Company of Chicago, Illinois, was founded in 1899 and sold vehicles until 1919. One model in 1903 was made to look like a gasoline automobile by utilizing a false hood or "bonnet." With prices ranging up to $4,500, Woods did not achieve a large sales volume but the firm's longevity proved that it had a respectable following. The Woods 1915 model featured solid rubber tires and claimed a 40-mph (64 km/hr) top speed with maximum range (at cruising speeds) of up to 100 miles (160 km) per charge. One of their last vehicles was a 1917 gasoline-electric hybrid featuring a 4-cylinder engine and electric motor. A 20-mph (32 km/hr) cruising speed on electric power alone could be augmented by the gasoline power plant to produce speeds of 25 mph (40 km/hr) in combination.

The Buffalo Electric Carriage Company of Buffalo, New York, built automobiles in various

Photo courtesy of the Museum of Transport, Glasgow

1899 MADELVIC ELECTRIC BROUGHAM
The Madelvic Motor Carriage Co. of Edinburgh, Scotland, produced this unusual model which featured exceptional coachwork. A small fifth wheel located behind the front carriage wheels supplied power to the ground. The entire 3-wheel front half of the vehicle could be attached to conventional horsedrawn vehicles. The company produced vehicles only until 1900.

1896 RIKER ELECTRIC THREE WHEELER

Andrew L. Riker produced this two-passenger tricycle from 1896 through 1898. Batteries were located under the seat and an 8-to-1 reduction gear-driven rear wheel eliminated the need for a differential.

In 1900 Riker's torpedo racer established records for electric cars including the mile in 1 minute, 46 seconds.

Riker produced vehicles which ranged from two-seater runabouts to heavy trucks. In 1900 Riker merged with the Electric Vehicle Company.

Photo courtesy of the Henry Ford Museum, Dearborn, Michigan

THE 1904 KRIÉGER

The 1904 Kriéger electric brougham of France featured power steering, four-wheel brakes and front-wheel drive. Kriégers were produced from 1897 to 1909; some later models used gasoline-powered generators to supplement battery energy.

In 1909, Kriéger patented a gas turbine-electric with rear wheel drive, but was forced into bankruptcy before the vehicle could be produced.

Photo courtest of Photo Hutin Compiegne, Paris

1897 HEADLAND ELECTRIC DOGCART
The Headland Electric Storage Battery Company of London, England, produced batteries and vehicles from 1897 to 1900.

1917 WOODS DUAL POWER 12-HP COUPE
This vehicle had an electric motor and a 12-hp, 4-cylinder Continental gasoline engine. Maximum speed for electric power was 20 mph (32 km/hr) and 35 mph (56 km/hr) using both engine and motor.
    The Woods Motor Vehicle Company of Chicago, Illinois, produced a variety of electrics from 1899 to 1919.

Photo courtesy of The National Motor Museum, England

Photo courtesy of The Henry Ford Museum, Dearborn, Michigan

1907 ELECTROMOBILE
The British Electromobile Company of London produced vehicles from 1901 to 1920.

Photo courtesy of
the National Motor Museum,
England

Photo courtesy of the National Motor Museum, England

QUEEN ALEXANDRIA AND HER 1901 COLUMBIA ELECTRIC.

km/hr). The road conditions of the day did not allow for high speeds. Cities were congested, therefore the top speed of electrics was perfectly acceptable.

The phenomena of overcrowding, congestion, and traffic jams are not indigenous to our times. Studies from the early part of this century indicate there may have been more traffic jams and congestion in the center of large cities then, than there are today. The combination of gasoline, horsedrawn, steam, and electric vehicles, inadequate streets, and the absence of proper traffic controls caused unbelievable tieups. (But then, for that matter, there were traffic jams in ancient Rome during the reign of Julius Caesar.)

Women were the champions of the electric automobile of the past. Comfortably positioned at the tiller of her dependable, quiet, and stately electric carriage, the lady driver could entertain an entire parlorful of her friends while traveling to her destination. Her vehicle was replete with plush interior, and exhibited only the most discreet road manners. The absence of the brutal and dangerous hand-cranked starter made the electric appealing to the genteel trade.

Electric vehicles flourished in cities where the streets were paved and the trips short, and in areas devoid of mud-tracked, hilly terrain and uncivilized driving conditions. The cities were the domain of the early electrics because the cities had electricity and in addition, many wealthy patrons who were the primary users of electric vehicles.

THE DEPARTURE OF THE ELECTRIC CAR

The causes of the disappearance of the early electric automobile were complex and totally devastating. Many factors led to its downfall, the most important of which was the perfection of a device that was composed of all the elements of the electric car itself. The inventor was Charles F. Kettering; the year, 1911; the invention, the automobile starter motor.

Kettering's early experience as an engineer for National Cash Register Company allowed him to produce an electric motor system to open cash register drawers. When asked by Henry M. Leland of the Cadillac Motor Company to develop an easier method of starting cars, Kettering applied the technology of the cash register motor to the automobile.

price categories from 1901 to 1906. Their light two-seater had a range of 75 miles (120 km) per charge. Prices ranged from $1,650 to $5,000 for six-seater models. Buffalo cars were later manufactured by Babcock from 1906 to 1912.

The Milburn Company of Toledo, Ohio, was one of the most successful manufacturers. Over 7,000 Milburns were sold from 1914 to as late as 1927. They included conventional models such as the five-passenger brougham. The 1919 Milburn limousine, and several other models, were designed to appear as gasoline automobiles to the extent that they not only had a hood but also incorporated a simulated radiator.

The year of 1912 was most prolific for electrics. Nearly 34,000 electric cars were registered, with scores of trucks and commercial vehicles to boot.

Early electric "town automobiles" had speeds of about 20 to 30 miles per hour (32-48

The automotive starter is a simple device, yet in 1911 there was not one successful, practical solution. Engineers had been working on the problem since the invention of the automobile. More than 25 years of hand cranking cars had passed. Many engineers argued that if an electric motor could be developed that would spin an internal combustion engine, it would weigh about 135 pounds and require several hundred pounds of batteries, (the payload of the vehicle itself).

But Kettering didn't look at it that way. He merely considered the problem and reasoned that a very small motor, over-loaded several times its capacity, could put out enough power to crank an engine for a brief period if it were allowed to cool between uses. The technique worked, much to the astonishment of the scientific community.

The new gasoline-powered automobiles with electric starters attracted the female driver who, until then, had relied on the "easy-to-drive" electric. This eliminated a major part of the market for the electric car.

Another man with an idea finished the electric car off for good. The man was Henry Ford. His mass-produced Model T's, originally priced at $850 in 1909, were selling for $260 in 1925. The Model T comprised over 40% of American motor car sales and records show that half of the cars on the road were "tin lizzies." The low price of the "T" enabled many people to purchase an automobile for the first time. The irony of this story is that of the 15 million Model T's sold during its reign, virtually every one had a hand-crank starter.

The lure of the countryside provided a market that was ripe for the gasoline vehicle which could extend its range indefinitely by merely storing or carrying more fuel. The gasoline automobile encroached upon the domain of the electrics because its range was double or triple that of an electric at a fraction of the cost.

The early electric car continued to plod along and eventually faded out because it became an anachronism. And, while talented designers used their imagination to build electric vehicles of the highest caliber, they had to stand by and watch the world go by while patiently awaiting new technology. To an extent, we are still waiting for that technology to catch up with the gasoline automobile.

In 1899, general scientific opinion was that batteries would become more efficient. Study was ongoing and scientists considered it a matter of time before a lightweight energy system would be invented. The electric vehicle industry waited with great optimism in the same way we are waiting today, 79 years later, for the arrival of a "superbattery".

The final blow to the electric car was that it could not appeal to the rural dwellers because they had no electricity. Although Thomas Edison's inventions electrified cities in the 1870's, rural electricity was sparse until well into the 1920's, 30's and 40's.

How primitive was the early electric automobile? In a recent road test conducted by *Machine Design Magazine,* a 1915 Detroit Electric was tested. Compared with modern electric cars, it did quite well. It was, in fact, recommended "Best Buy."

The interior, replete with overstuffed seats and tieback curtains, was reminiscent of grandma's parlor. Powered by twelve 6-volt batteries and a 5.5 horsepower motor, it produced an 80-mile (129 km) range, using large diameter, high-pressure tires designed for the electric automobiles of the day. A top speed of 25 mph (40 km/hr) could quietly be achieved. The car carried five passengers, two of whom sat in chairs facing rearward and three in a main seat facing forward. Although the seating position design was more of a concession to pleasant parlor conversation, the visibility for the driver was excellent. The high, flat-pane windows were designed for full visibility in all directions even

Photo courtesy of Gilbert Heinrich

1915 DETROIT ELECTRIC
This elegantly-restored 1915 Detroit Electric belongs to Mr. Gilbert Heinrich of Electric Vehicle Associates, Cleveland, Ohio. A top speed of 25 mph (40 km/hr) and range of 80 miles (129 km) per charge were noted.

ELECTRIC SURREY IN OPERATION.

ELECTRIC SURREY CONSTRUCTED ON "THE RIKER SYSTEM," SHOWING DETAILS OF WORKING PARTS

when carrying a full complement of passengers. The Detroit Electrics displayed the excellent quality of a finely made machine. Although fitted with modern batteries, it is basically as it was originally, in an era when designers knew how to build electric cars. Let us hope that we will see some of our 1979 models "street-working" in sixty years or so.

Today, as large corporations and positive governmental forces begin to work, we will begin acquiring the technology our forefathers so desperately desired. The electric car today has an opportunity to succeed as never before.

The following companies have produced electric vehicles:

D = Germany   F = France   US = U.S.A.   B = Belgium   CH = Switzerland
A = Austria   GB = Great Britain   J = Japan   NL = Holland

1893-1900

Jeantaud (F)—1893-1906

Morris & Salom (US)—1895-1897

Riker (US)—1896-1902

Columbia (US)—1897-1913

Headland (GB)—1897-1900

Krieger (F)—1897-1909

General Electric (US)—1898-1899

Jenatzy (B)—1898-1903

Lohner (Lohner-Porsche Electric Cars) (A)—1898-1906

Madelvic (GB)—1898-1900

Waverly (US)—1898-1903

American Electric (US)—1899-1902

Baker (US)—1899-1916

B.G.S. (F)—1899-1906

Cleveland (US)—1899-1901

Eastman (US)—1899-1902

Henschel (D)—1899-1906

Scheele (D)—1899-1910

Woods (US)—1899-1919

1900-1915

Cardinet (F)—1900-1906

National (US)—1900-1904

Electromotion (F)—1900-1909

Bachelle (US)—1901-1902

Buffalo (US)—1901-1906

City & Suburban (GB)—1901-1905

Electromobile (GB)—1901-1920

Studebaker (US)—1902-1912

Tribelhorn (CH)—1902-1920

Borland (US)—1903-1916

Pope-Waverly (US)—1903-1907

Regina (F)—1903-1908

Fritchle (US)—1904-1917

Rauch & Lang (US)—1905-1928

Silvertown (GB)—1905-1910

Babcock (US)—1906-1912

Siemens-Schuckert (D)—1906-1910

Bailey (US)—1907-1915

B.E.F. (D)—1907-1913

Detroit Electric (US)—1907-1938

Waverly (US)—1908-1914

Broc (US)—1909-1916

Grinnell (US)—1910-1913

Kimball (US)—1910-1912

Ohio (US)—1910-1918

Hupp-Yeats (US)—1911-1919

Argo (US)—1912-1914

Church-Field (US)—1912-1913

Flanders (US)—1912-1913

Tiffany (US)—1913-1914

Flanders (US)—1914-1915

Milburn (US)—1914-1922

Chicago (US)—1915-1916

World War I 1914-1918

S.B. (D)—1920-1924

Post-World War I

Automatic (US)—1921

Chelsea (GB)—1922

Elektric (D)—1922-1924

World War II 1939-1945

Chapeaux (F)—1940-1941

During World War II

Le Dauphin (F)—1941-1942

Faure (F)—1941-1947

Stela (F)—1941-1944

After World War II

Tama (J)—1947-1951

B.M.A. Hazelcar (GB)—1952-1957

NOTE: Some manufacturers produced many models for a number of years. The 1913 Waverley, for example, offered 11 models of trucks and cars. The Studebaker Company of South Bend, Indiana, produced over 1,800 electrics from 1902 to 1912, one of which was specially designed for the personal use of Thomas A. Edison.

More Luxury–New Conveniences–Greater Comfort in the Magnificent New Baker Coupé

The mere announcement of the magnificent New Baker Coupe resulted in the sale of hundreds of cars throughout the country, even before the first lot had received the final touches in their careful course through the big Baker plant.

There could be no more emphatic proof that this handsome model—the latest creation by the oldest, foremost and largest electric car builders in the country—fully meets the demand for a thoroughly stylish, yet conservative, coupe. It is a big, roomy motor car, with full limousine back, longer wheel base, graceful, low-hung body lines and new hoods of French design.

REVOLVING FRONT SEATS are one of the innovations introduced in this Baker Model. These permit the occupants to face forward or turn about. Easy view of the road is possible from the rear seat because of the exceptionally low front and front quarter windows.

Either Lever or Wheel Steer

The former from rear seat, the latter from left front seat (with controlling lever attached to steering mast). In every detail this new Baker is a car of supreme convenience and luxury.

Baker luxury endures, because the car itself was built *first*; the luxury was added afterward. With Baker beauty is unquestioned mechanical excellence—the kind that gives the car its long life; its remarkable ability to climb hills and to stand up under the hardest service, always at a *lower cost of upkeep* than any other electric.

THE BAKER MOTOR VEHICLE COMPANY, CLEVELAND, OHIO

Builders also of Baker Electric Trucks   CANADA: The Baker Motor Vehicle Company of Canada, Ltd., Walkerville, Ont.

Photo courtesy of the National Motor Museum, England

BAKER ELECTRICS
(facing page)

The Baker Electric Company (1899-1916), later Baker, Rauch & Lang, Cleveland, Ohio, was one of the most important electric vehicle producers in the U.S.

The firm was formed by Walter C. Baker, a pioneer in electric vehicle development. As early as 1893, Baker had assisted in the building of the "Electrobat" for the World's Columbian Exposition in Chicago. He was also associated with the development of ball bearings for automotive use, and engineered the lightweight alloy axles for the Model T Ford.

The accomplishments of Walter Baker are manifest, from his experimental Baker "Torpedo" racer of 1902 to the myriad of dependable production electrics he provided Americans. His death at 87 in 1955 did not erase the name of Baker from the roster of electric vehicle manufacturers—electric forklifts are produced today the the Baker Industrial Truck Division of Otis Elevator Corporation, Cleveland, Ohio.

The Rauch & Lang Company was active from 1905 to 1928. In 1916 they merged with Baker to form Baker, Rauch & Lang. After 1922 the vehicles were called Raulangs.

1922 CHELSEA ELECTRIC COUPE

This model had the distinction of having a simulated radiator in a front grill assembly. The Wandsworth Engineering Works of London was the manufacturer.

1913 BAILEY MODEL F PHAETON

This model had the distinction of re-sembling a gaso-line-powered auto-mobile more than an electric. The top speed was 20 mph (32 km/hr); range was from 80 to 100 miles (129 to 161 km) per charge. The S. R. Bailey Co. of Amesbury, Mass., produced electric cars from 1907 to 1915. Today, the Bailey Company produces precision rolled products.

Photo courtesy of the Henry Ford Museum, Dearborn, Michigan

1919 MILBURN ELECTRIC

The Milburn Wagon Company of Toledo, Ohio, produced over 7,000 electric auto-mobiles between 1914 and 1922.

Photo courtesy of the Museum of Science & Industry, Chicago

1913 COMMERCIAL TRUCK

Photo courtesy of the Smithsonian Institute

EARLY COMMERCIAL VEHICLES

Imagine that you are a truck fleet owner faced with the proposition of changing your vehicles to either electric or gasoline. The trucks in your metropolitan area are about 50% electric and 50% gasoline-powered. Some friends suggest that gasoline would be the more economically feasible route, yet others proclaim electrics as the wave of the future. The question is difficult and you weigh your decision carefully. This is not the year 2000, but 1905. It actually happened.

From 1900 to 1920, thousands of electric trucks and delivery vehicles were in use because of the unique nature of the driving public of the day. Delivery men, usually accustomed to horse and carriage, found the gasoline vehicles difficult to operate. Complicated gear reductions and elaborate transmissions proved confusing to men whose only mechanical experience was that of holding the reins and speaking to the engine. Electric trucks had simple controls and lacked the smoke, noise, and vibrations of the gasoline

versions. When speeds of 8 or 10 mph (13 or 16 km/hr) were commonplace, roads were half-paved and deliveries were largely local (leaving cross-country freight to the railroading industry), the electrics thrived. When all of these advantages disappeared, the electric truck was soon to follow.

The assortment of electric commercial vehicles in the 1898 to 1918 period was a formidable group indeed. Some were fire engines, taxicabs, garbage collectors, tractors, lightpole repairers, heavy haulers, train switchers, crane carriers, freight handlers—but the largest group was light multistop delivery vans.

The "van," an English term for a lightweight truck, was and *is* an ideal use of electric power. To cite an example: a 1915 Lansden van could run 93 miles (150 km) a day, making 100 stops or deliveries on a single charge. It weighed 2,460 pounds (1116 kg) and could carry a 2,000-pound (907 kg) payload. It was equipped with an Edison, nickel-iron battery system that weighed

The unusual strap-steel drive shaft assembly of an early G.M.C. electric van.

A COMMERCIAL ELECTRIC "TRIMMER'S WAGON."

1,200 pounds (544 kg). This type of vehicle was used by department stores and express delivery companies in New York, Chicago, and other large cities. Some vans were used 14 to 18 hours a day and charged at night with large 40- amp battery chargers.

In 1915, one New York firm alone used 350 delivery vans. No fewer than 2,300 electric vehicles with over 100 garages for recharging existed in New York in that year. Over 45 firms had "fleets" of 10 units or more. Berlin had almost 1,000 electrics, mostly post office trucks and taxicabs.

Although Paris used electrics for garbage and refuse service, and England utilized both British and German electric postal service trucks, it was New York City with seven million dollars worth of electrics and equipment that led the field.

Reliability was the keynote. Greater reliability than the gasoline truck, especially for 80% of city deliveries, made the electric attractive. Low maintenance, combined with a minimum amount of "down time" enabled many electrics to show an average of 297 days in service out of a 300-day work year.

FIFTY TWO-TON BAKER ELECTRIC DELIVERY VANS
These vans were used by the American Express Company, one of two hundred companies using fleets of Bakers in 1912. They were never equalled for economy or dependabililty.

A GERMAN ELECTRIC TAXICAB, WITH ROOF BAGGAGE RACK.

The names of some of the truck manufacturers during the prolific 1898-1915 period were Waverly, Baker, Milburn, Riker, Orwell, Detroit, G.M.C., G.V., Commercial, Landsen, Buffalo, Clayton Couple-Gear, Walker, Urban, Ward, Voltacar, Guy, Eldrige, and Field, to name a few.

Early electric trucks, it must be understood, traveled at extremely slow speeds. A five-ton truck would travel at only seven miles per hour—slightly faster than walking speed—and carried 10,000 pounds (4,530 kg) for 35 miles (56 km) on one battery charge. The lightest trucks, the 1/2 ton variety, traveled at 12 mph (19 km/hr), with a load capacity of 1,000 pounds (453 kg) and a 45 mile (72 km) range per charge. Although a 45 mile (72 km) range for a lightweight van would be acceptable by today's standards, the 12 mph (19 km) top speed would be absurd. The vehicles of that day did not require high speeds in heavy city traffic situations. However, when the speed and distance requirements became higher, the electric truck disappeared.

Solid rubber tires were preferred for the electric trucks of that day. Manufacturers dis-

AN EARLY GENERAL VEHICLE
ELECTRIC DELIVERY VAN.

AN EARLY WARD
TWO-TON ELECTRIC TRUCK.

AN EARLY WAVERLY ELECTRIC TRUCK.

couraged the use of pneumatic tires because of their unreliability.

The earliest electric trucks were understandably primitive; although the Riker of 1898 had the appearance of a large "horseless" covered wagon, it nevertheless incorporated dual-geared rear wheels and a rear gate for loading, much like the modern trucks of today.

The Commercial electric truck of America was a very rugged, diversified carrier. One truck was reported to be used daily for over fifty years. The Couple-Gear truck was used for heavy hauling, fire engines, garbage trucks and a variety of uses, including a four-wheel drive truck fitted for passenger use. One model of

AN EARLY WARD ELECTRIC DELIVERY VAN.

THE INTERNAL VIEW OF A COUPLE-GEAR TRUCK WHEEL SHOWING THE BUILT-IN MOTOR.

THE STEERING SHAFT AND ELECTRIC CONTROLLER OF AN EARLY COMMERCIAL TRUCK.

this type had four-wheel drive, four-wheel steering and "power steering." To turn left, power was applied to the right front wheel, thus pushing the vehicle to the left. This was made possible by the use of a sophisticated geared motor built into the hub of the wheels. Another model had a four-cylinder gasoline engine powering a generator, eliminating the batteries and the transmission, while not complicating the ease of operation. This was one of America's most effective electrics built between 1910 and 1918.

The G.M.C. Electric Wagon's unique drive train used a long strap of spring steel to connect the motor to the differential, thus elimin-

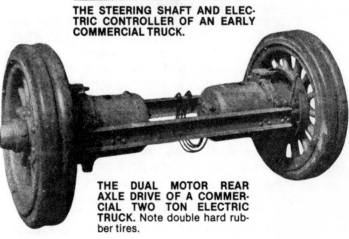

THE DUAL MOTOR REAR AXLE DRIVE OF A COMMERCIAL TWO TON ELECTRIC TRUCK. Note double hard rubber tires.

ating the drive shaft and universal joints normally used with this type of drive. The steel strap created a buffer effect that eliminated jerky start-ups when power was applied.

The early electric truck simply could not meet the needs of the trucking industry, especially when cross country hauling became necessary.

But even so, locally-used electric commercial vehicles do exist today. There are over 100,000 electric fork lifts in use in the United States alone. Britain delivers milk, eggs and other perishables in small electric vans called "milk floats," which number upwards of 50,000. And the electric golf cart is so uniquely suited for its job that it is predominant in its field.

RECENT HISTORY

In America, during 1966 and 1967, General Motors, Ford, and American Motors were developing modern electric passenger car prototypes. More than a dozen of these vehicles have been produced and demonstrated. This resurgence of electric vehicles interest followed in the wake of statements made by several influential public officials condemning the combustion- engined vehicle as a menace to public health.

General Motors brought out two prototype demonstration vehicles, namely a Chevrolet Corvair called the ElectroVair and a GMC electric fuel cell van called the ElectroVan. The batteries GM selected were silver-zinc with extremely short cycle life and extraordinary high cost. The fuel cell for the ElectroVan had to be replenished every 125 miles (201 km) and was complicated as well as bulky. The fuel cell required a fluid electrolyte which was pumped through the cells. The ElectroVair's range was only 80 miles (129 km) per charge coupled with an extremely low number of potential recharge cycles. The batteries for the ElectroVair II were priced at $15,000 in 1967, which is equivalent to about $30,000 today.

The ElectroVair I was built on a 1964 Corvair body and chassis; the ElectroVair II was built on a 1966 Corvair body and chassis. The 680-pound (308 kg) battery pack powered a 115-horsepower alternating current, induction motor which required oil for cooling because of a 13,000 rpm motor speed. Problems with the vehicle, as described by GM, were short range, short battery life, long recharge time, heavy weight and bulky size of the battery and drive

systems, costly components and materials, difficult cooling requirements, safety problems with lack of engine braking as a possible hazard, and radio and TV interference.

The General Motors ElectroVairs are an example of an effort to produce high technology with no regard to practicality. The silver-zinc batteries were unrealistic, to say the least, as an inclusion into an electric vehicle. The 13,000 rpm motor, which was of an alternating current design, did not provide engine braking of any kind. This posed a safety hazard. Cooling of the motor, components and unusual complexity of design marred this valiant attempt to produce a usable vehicle.

The 1966 GMC HandiVan which was converted to produce the ElectroVan utilized a fuel cell system. The hydrogen-oxygen fuel cells used were extremely bulky and required that a hydrogen and oxygen tank be fitted into the back of the van. Basically, motor and controls were the same as the ElectroVair II.

The illustration shows the complexity of the first fuel-cell-powered van ever to be built. The 7,100-pound (3219 kg) ElectroVan powered by a 125 hp AC motor, had a top speed of 70 mph (112 km/hr) and a range of 100 to 150 miles (161 to 241 km).

Among the problems encountered by GM with the ElectroVan were heavy weight and large volume, short lifetime, costly components and materials, complicated and lengthy start-up and shut-down procedures, gas bleeds and gas leaks, complexity of the three separate fluid systems (electrolyte, hydrogen, and oxygen), a long list of safety problems, possible collision hazards, hydrogen leaks, electrolyte leaks, high voltages, and so on. Perhaps this is why we see very little fuel cell research activity for electric vehicles. The system is too expensive and complicated.

Besides the ElectroVair and ElectroVan, General Motors produced some special-purpose urban electric cars in 1969. These cars are generally acknowledged as excellent small-vehicle designs. The GM512 Series car uses one basic body with three separate experimental power plants. One is a battery-electric, another is a hybrid gasoline-electric, and a third is a gasoline-engine vehicle. The two- passenger vehicle has an overall length of 86.3 inches (220 cm) and a width of 56 inches (145 cm). Access to the vehicle is from the front, much like the BMW Isetta, which was a small German car popular in the 50's.

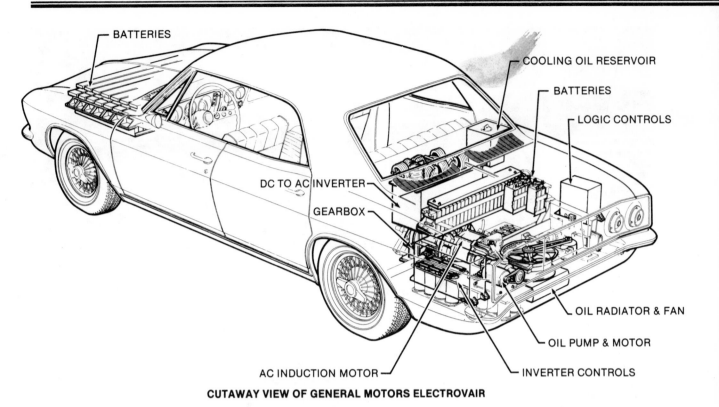

CUTAWAY VIEW OF GENERAL MOTORS ELECTROVAIR

- BATTERIES
- COOLING OIL RESERVOIR
- BATTERIES
- LOGIC CONTROLS
- DC TO AC INVERTER
- GEARBOX
- OIL RADIATOR & FAN
- OIL PUMP & MOTOR
- AC INDUCTION MOTOR
- INVERTER CONTROLS

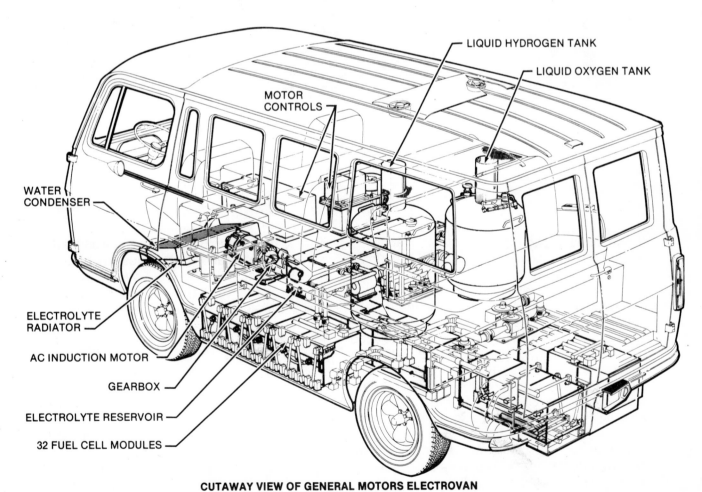

CUTAWAY VIEW OF GENERAL MOTORS ELECTROVAN

- LIQUID HYDROGEN TANK
- LIQUID OXYGEN TANK
- MOTOR CONTROLS
- WATER CONDENSER
- ELECTROLYTE RADIATOR
- AC INDUCTION MOTOR
- GEARBOX
- ELECTROLYTE RESERVOIR
- 32 FUEL CELL MODULES

This gasoline-electric hybrid is one of three experimental 512 series of special-purpose cars developed by General Motors Engineering Staff in the late 60's. Its power system consists of a 12-cubic-inch gasoline engine coupled with a series DC electric motor through an electro-magnetic clutch. It runs either in electric or hybrid mode.

Photo courtesy of General Motors Corp.

The battery pack consisted of seven light-weight 85 amp-hour, 47-pound (21 kg) units. This vehicle used an SCR controller and a Delco-Remy DC series-wound motor, capable of producing 8-1/2 horsepower. The hybrid 512 Series vehicle used a gasoline engine and electric motor combination. Electric drive was used zero to 10 mph (16 km): At speeds of 10-13 mph both power plants operated together. At speeds greater than 13 mph, (21 km) the gasoline engine was used exclusively. The gasoline engine was a 2-cylinder, 11.7 cubic inch (195 cc) displacement variety of a rather inefficient design. Attempts had been made to modify the engine by increasing the compression ratio, but the unit would not withstand the excess power.

The 90-volt, 20-ampere alternator was belt-driven at engine speed to recharge the battery, or conventional 115-volt AC outlets could be used. The constant-speed fuel economy was 45 to 50 miles per gallon (19.5 to 21.2 km/l). In the electric mode, the range and speed varied from 5.2 miles (8.3 km) at 30 mph, to 9 miles (14 km) at 10 mph (16 km). Unfortunately, more than one acceleration run every 2.5 miles (4 km) would result in battery depletion.

In fact, the top speed of the electric was 45 mph (72 km/hr) and the top speed of the hybrid was only 40 mph (64 km/hr). The electric was also faster in acceleration.

This vehicle was experimental and cannot be considered the culmination of high technology.

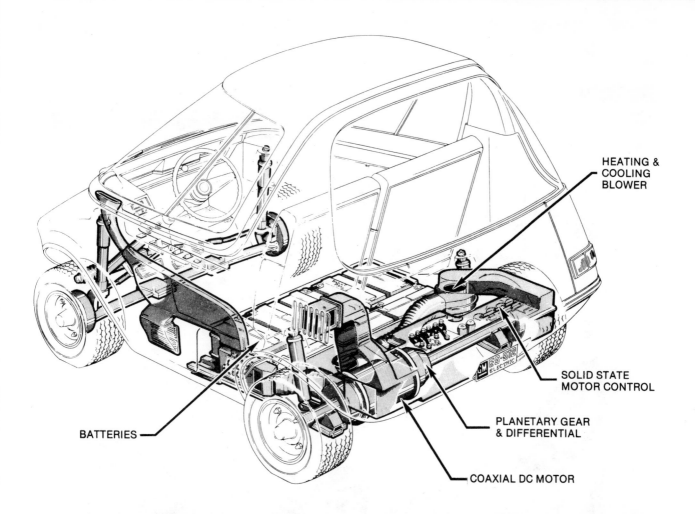

HEATING &
COOLING
BLOWER

SOLID STATE
MOTOR CONTROL

PLANETARY GEAR
& DIFFERENTIAL

COAXIAL DC MOTOR

BATTERIES

THE G.M. SERIES 512 CARS

Photo courtesy of General Motors Corporation

The XP512E electric car is powered by 12 maintenance-free lead acid traction batteries. Features
include a DC motor, solid-state motor control and a canopy which could be removed.

FORD COMUTA
The Ford Motor Company contribution to the "volt-rush" of the late 60's was the Comuta which was developed by the Ford of Britain Research Staff. The vehicle was only 80″ (203 cm) long.

Photo courtesy of Ford Motor Company

A modern Honda Civic or Toyota could approach the mileage of this hybrid and maintain complete road-worthiness and meet all safety requirements to boot.

FORD

The Ford Motor Company announced the development of an experimental electric car in June, 1967. The Ford Comuta was designed by Ford of Britain's Research Staff. The vehicle

is 80 inches in overall length, which is less than half the length of its contemporary, the 1967 Ford Mustang. The photo shows the chassis with batteries in position.

AMERICAN MOTORS AMITRON

While General Motors and Ford were building prototypes in the 1960's, American Motors introduced a very sophisticated prototype called the Amitron. This sleek, efficient, teardrop-

FORD COMUTA

shaped coupe had a 50-mph (80 km/hr) cruising speed. A maximum range of 150 miles (241 km) per charge was based on moderate cruising speed.

The battery systems used in the Amitron were developed by Gulton Industries, a major battery manufacturer. Two different types of batteries were used: lithium-nickel fluoride and nickel-cadmium bipolar units. The two lithium batteries had a storage capacity of up to ten times as much energy as conventional lead-acid batteries of the same size.

The two nickel-cadmium bipolar batteries provided the energy reserve to allow acceleration of up to 50 mph (80 km/hr) in 20 seconds. Also the bipolar batteries could be recharged from the lithium batteries while the car was in a cruising mode. The advantage of the nickel-cadmium units was 1,000 recharge cycles over a three year period. A 4-hour recharge capability helped make this comparatively lightweight, 200-pound (91 kg) battery supply very attractive.

The vehicle also incorporated a regenerative

THE AMITRON

Photo courtesy of American Motors Corporation

The American Motors' entry to the electric car development program of the late 60's, designated the "Amitron."

This three-passenger prototype had a Gulton lithium battery system, regenerative braking and solid-state controls.

A range of 150 miles (241 km) per charge, and speeds of up to 50 mph (80 km/hr) were claimed. Acceleration was 0 to 50 mph (0 to 80 km/hr) in 20 seconds.

Two lithium-nickel flouride batteries* rated at 150 watt-hours per lb (331 watt hours per kg) used with two nickel-cadmium batteries in combination. Battery weight was only 200 lbs (91 kg).

braking system that could recapture part of the lost energy of braking into electric storage.

Another interesting aspect of the vehicle was weight-saving, air-filled seats which could be lowered to increase cargo carrying capacity. Also featured were helicopter-style instrumentation behind the steering wheel, a clam-shell-type door which when open exposed the entire roof via a counterbalanced pivot system, and bumpers made of vinyl-rubber that could absorb impact and return to their original shape.

The Amitron project was not further developed, in spite of the fact that it was very well received publicly when it was introduced in 1968. The expensive batteries and other factors contributed to the decision of AMC to suspend testing of this vehicle.

*Batteries will be discussed in detail in Chapter 4.

"THE GREAT ELECTRIC CAR RACE"

One recent "historical event" in electric vehicle development occurred in August, 1968. The event was "The Great Electric Car Race," conducted by students from the California Institute of Technology (CalTech) in Pasadena and students from the Massachusetts Institute of Technology (MIT) in Cambridge. The object of the race was for the MIT electrically-converted Chevrolet 1968 Corvair (borrowed from General Motors), to reach the CalTech campus before the CalTech converted 1958 Volkswagen Microbus, called the "Voltswagen," could reach the MIT campus.

The CalTech vehicle was owned by Wally Rippel, a graduate student in physics. It was supplied with twenty lead-cobalt batteries worth about $600, weighing 95 pounds each, and pro-

CAL TECH ELECTRIC VAN

duced by the Electric Fuel Propulsion Company of Ann Arbor, Michigan. E.F.P. Company's president, Mr. Robert Aronson, had also made arrangements for some mid-trip recharging stations. The CalTech car was accompanied by another ten- year-old vehicle, a 1958 Chevrolet, which towed a portable generator trailer for emergency recharging. There were five other vehicles which assisted the CalTech entry besides the 220-volt generator vehicle.

The MIT vehicle was a bit more sophisticated, besides being ten years newer. It carried 2,000 lbs. (907 kg) of nickel-cadmium batteries worth about $20,000 and supplied by Gulton Industries. The MIT Corvair was a laboratory model which had not been driven until shortly before the race. In fact, a pre-race trial run almost burned up their batteries. The MIT vehicle had an advanced, experimental, motor weighing 80 pounds (36 kg) and developing 30 horsepower. The permanent magnet motor was equipped with a high power, solid state control system much more advanced than the CalTech

vehicle. The CalTech vehicle used a 20 horsepower traction motor such as the type used in forklifts. Both vehicles had the same range per charge, but the Corvair traveled five to ten miles (8 to 16 km) per hour faster and a recharge took 15 minutes versus 45 minutes for the Voltswagen. Both vehicles consumed about $25.00 worth of electricity on the entire trip. But the trip was fraught with obstacles:

1. MIT proceeded without much difficulty across the Midwest after starting the race August 26, 1968. The only real problem the first few days was the overheating which occurred in the nickel-cadmium battery pack. This problem was solved by packing ice around the batteries and resorting to a four hour charge.

2. The second day for CalTech brought crew problems when one member contracted the mumps and had to be replaced. Also, the armature of the motor disintegrated about 400 miles (644 km) out, which resulted in a 23-hour wait for a new motor shipped by air to Phoenix,

Arizona, from the Electric Fuel Propulsion Company.

3. The CalTech vehicle was experiencing overheating as well, while recharging the lead-cobalt battery. The recharging rate had to be slowed down, which lost precious time that could have been used for driving.

4. One member of the CalTech crew lost a contact lens which cost forty minutes of driving time. The lens was not found.

5. The MIT car caught fire when being re-charged at Elkhart, Indiana. The fire was put out quickly, but damage caused a ten-hour delay.

6. The MIT car had problems with overheating in Springfield, Illinois. The method for cooling motor overheating problems was to pour water on the motor.

7. The CalTech car blew out three diodes in its recharging circuit. More ice had to be continuously applied to batteries, using a siphon-hose purchased in McLean, Texas, to remove water from the battery enclosure.

8. The MIT car reached California first, but crew members did not like the charging setup at Newbury, so they decided to tow their vehicle to the next point, Victorville. One member of the crew, however, forgot to take the vehicle out of low gear, and the electric motor burned up by being towed at 65 mph (105 km/hr). The MIT car had to be towed directly to CalTech, bypassing the last two charge points, in order to reach the finish line.

9. The CalTech car reached Cambridge on September 4, without having to be towed at all.

10. The winning time was 210 hours and 3 minutes for the 3,300 mile (5309 km) cross-country race period. Although the MIT car arrived in Pasadena 7-1/2 days after the start, with the CalTech entry coming into Cambridge 37 hours and 20 minutes later, the CalTech entry was voted the winner after certain penalties were deducted. These penalties involved deductions for towing time, recharging with a portable generator between official charging stations and time lost replacing parts. In effect, the tortoise had beaten the hare, and the tortoise made it on its own power. The entire trip was judged on both sides by representatives from Machine Design magazine. A good deal of press coverage and public participation made this event the circus that one would expect it to be.

At this point, we must review a few details. The electric vehicle was never intended for cross-country use. The pollution in the middle of Arizona is not high enough to warrant much concern for emission control. However, the test that was made showed public interest in electric vehicles, and pointed out the improvements necessary to produce an efficient product. The batteries, produced by Electric Fuel Propulsion Company, have been revised and improved in the last ten years, as have solid state speed controls and motor systems. The electric vehicle as a commuter car and commercial truck for urban use is still a very attractive vehicle. While we may not see thousands of them running on the highways, we will definitely see millions of them on our city streets in the 21st century.

During the 1970's programs were initiated to develop electrics in Europe, Japan and the United States. The motivating force which caused the return of the electric was due in part to the Arab Oil Embargo of late 1973. Since then, a concerted effort on the part of manufacturers in all countries has developed many prototypes and a number of limited-production vehicles.

ELECTRIC VEHICLE SPEED RECORD HISTORY

The dominance of early electric vehicles was evidenced by the fact that in 1899, the world's fastest vehicles were electric. Two pioneers in electric vehicle development, both Frenchmen, Charles Jeantaud and Camille Jenatzy, fought to achieve the world's speed record. Jeantaud set the record of 39.24 mph (63.1 km/hr) in December of 1898. Jenatzy a month later returned with a speed of 41 mph (66 km/hr), only to be beaten by Jeantaud with 43.69 mph (70 km/hr). The final speed record of 68.8 mph (110 km/hr) was attained by Jenatzy in the "La-Jamais Contente" ("The Never Satisfied") in 1899. After each high speed run, the vehicle batteries were so heavily discharged that they were worthless. The battle that raged between these two Frenchmen made them popular heroes and further galvanized the stronghold of electric automobiles.

The great speed race was not the first en-

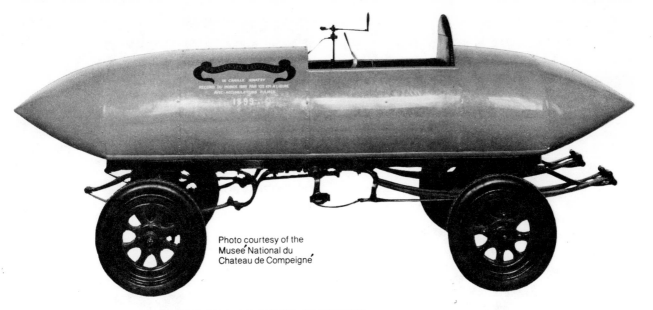

Photo courtesy of the
Musée National du
Chateau de Compeigné

JENATZY'S "LA JAMAIS CONTENTE"
The world's speed record holder in 1899, a bullet-shaped
electric race car. A speed of 68.8 mph (110 km/hr) captured
the record, yet the racer had a top speed, unofficially, of 75
mph (121 km/hr). "La Jamais Contente" means "The Never
Satisfied."

counter Jeantaud and Jenatzy had with each other. They had previously competed in the 1898 "Paris Motor Cab Trials," which was a test designed to determine the best manufacturer of Paris taxis. Jeantaud had won this demonstration with his taxi design. Both Jeantaud and Jenatzy produced electric vehicles commercially during the period of 1893 to 1906. Eventually, both turned their interest away from electric vehicles and began producing gasoline-powered automobiles in 1902.

In 1902, a Baker electric, racer, called the "Torpedo," recorded an unofficial speed on Staten Island Boulevard in New York of 78 mph (126 km/hr), after which it crashed. In 1904 a rebuilt version of the Torpedo, called "The Torpedo Kid," achieved 104 mph (167 km/hr) at Daytona, in the U.S.A.

A non-stop distance record in France was established by a 1901 Krieger which traveled 192 miles (310 km) on a single charge.

Formerly, the French B.G.S. Electric Car held the world's distance record for electrics of almost 180 miles per charge (262 km) in 1900.

The next speed record specifically designed for electric vehicles was set in 1968 by Jerry Kugel with a "flying mile" record of 138 mph (223 km/hr) in the Autolite Lead Wedge at Bonneville, Utah, U.S.A. The vehicle weighed about

one ton (1,015 kg) and was powered by a 120 horsepower AC motor. Lead-acid batteries supplied the power.

In August 1972, the Eagle-Picher "Silver Eagle" produced a flying mile record of 146.437 mph (237 km/hr), at Bonneville. The silver-zinc batteries were the same variety that were used in the "Lunar Rover." A 102 horsepower DC motor was used.

The world's land speed record for an electric-powered motorcycle was set by Mike Corbin on August 19, 1974, with a speed of 165.367 mph (266 km/hr). The silver-zinc batteries, developing 1,000 amps at 120 volts, pushed the "Quicksilver" to 171.102 mph (275.3 km/hr) during qualification. The vehicle measured nine feet in length and weighed over 700 pounds (408 kg). Power was supplied by two jet aircraft engine starter motors developing 100 horsepower each.

On August 23, 1974, the "Battery Box" of Roger Hedlund captured the flying mile and kilometer speed record at 175 mph (281.5 km/hr). The efficiency of the vehicle which used lead-acid batteries was very high. At 175 mph (281.5 km/hr) the vehicle consumed electricity at a rate equivalent to 55 miles per gallon (23.3 km/l) of gasoline.

Photo courtesy of John B. Newell

THE BATTERY BOX

Roger Hedlund's record holding electric car at the Bonneville Salt Flats, Utah, August 23, 1974.

Photo courtesy of Corbin-Gentry, Inc.

CORBIN-GENTRY "QUICK SILVER"

On August 19, 1974, the world's fastest electric motorcycle was driven by Mike Corbin at the Bonneville Salt Flats, Utah, U.S.A. The "Quicksilver" established a new record speed of 165.367 mph (266 km/hr) with a trap speed during time trials of 171.1 mph (275 km/hr). The vehicle was powered by Yardney; silver-zinc batteries supplied by the Yardney Electric Company, Pawcatuck, Conn.

Photo courtesy of Ford Motor Company

THE LEAD WEDGE

The Lead Wedge was built jointly by the Autolite Corporation and the Ford Motor Company for the 1968 Bonneville Salt Flats speed record. The chassis housing motor and batteries is shown in foreground. Fiberglass body shell is in background.

Photo courtesy of Eagle-Picher Company

EAGLE PICHER "SILVER EAGLE"

The Silver Eagle established 21 records for electrics—14 national and 7 international—at the Bonneville Salt Flats, Utah, U.S.A., in August, 1972.
   The vehicle had an unofficial top speed of 152.59 mph (245.5 km/hr).

THE LUNAR ROVERS

(An electric vehicle that was really out of this world.)

Photo courtesy of The Boeing Aerospace Company

Three "LRV," Lunar Roving Vehicles, were produced by the Boeing Aerospace Company under the direction of NASA, the U.S. National Aeronautic and Space Administration. The "Moon Buggies" accompanied the Apollo 15, 16 and 17 flights during 1971 and 1972.

The 462-lb (209-kg) Rovers carried up to four times their weight, or 1,606 lbs (728 kg) and performed in temperatures from −200 to +220 F (93 to 104C).

Features included: four-wheel steering with a 1/4-hp, series-wound motor at each wheel, lightweight aluminum chassis construction, woven wire wheels to reduce weight, and two unrechargeable 59-lb (27-kg) silver-zinc 36-V primary batteries, manufactured by the Eagle Picher Industries, Joplin, Missouri, rated at total of 242 amps. The Rovers carried television, communication equipment and navigational equipment.

A maximum range of 57 miles (92 km) and a top speed of 10 mph (16 km/hr) was possible, although range never exceeded 22 miles (35 km) and speed of 8 mph (13 km/hr).

The Lunar Rovers were carried on three Apollo missions and performed every function flawlessly. The program record ended with three successful missions in three attempts.

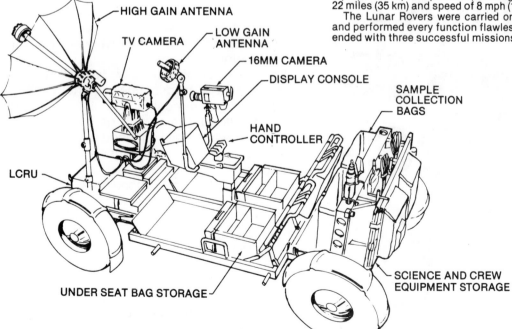

HIGH GAIN ANTENNA
TV CAMERA
LOW GAIN ANTENNA
16MM CAMERA
DISPLAY CONSOLE
SAMPLE COLLECTION BAGS
HAND CONTROLLER
LCRU
SCIENCE AND CREW EQUIPMENT STORAGE
UNDER SEAT BAG STORAGE

Fundamentals of Electricity

In the spirit of making this book an easy-to-read guide to electric vehicles, we will discuss electricity as simply as possible.

The word "electric" comes from a Greek word meaning "amber." Amber is a translucent mineral composed of fossilized resin. The ancient Greeks used the words "electric force" to refer to the mysterious forces of attraction and repulsion exhibited by amber when it was rubbed with a cloth.

For the sake of simplicity, we will use the following theory to describe electricity. When electricity flows through a wire, it is very much like water flowing through a garden hose. If a 50-foot garden hose is attached to a faucet and the faucet is turned on, water begins to flow. As the faucet is turned on and off, the water responds by flowing or stopping at the end of the 50-foot hose.

Water, flowing in a current, is affected by three factors:

1. Pressure
2. Rate of flow
3. Resistance to flow

Electric current running through a conductor exhibits similar characteristics:

1. Voltage

2. Current
3. Resistance

There are two types of electrical charges: positive and negative. A basic law of electricity is that like charges repel each other, and unlike charges attract each other. In other words, positive charges repel each other and negative charges repel each other, but negative and positive charges attract each other. Figure E-1.

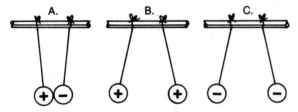

Figure E-1. **REACTION BETWEEN CHARGED BODIES**

In a battery, chemical action causes positive charges to collect on the positive terminal and negative charges to collect on the negative terminal. Because unlike charges attract, there is

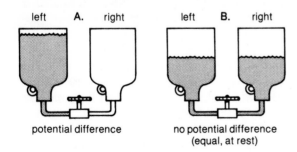

potential difference   no potential difference
                               (equal, at rest)

Figure E-2. **WATER ANALOGY OF DIFFERENCE IN ELECTRIC POTENTIAL**

A few seconds after you open the valve, the level of the water in the two bottles will be equal.

Before you opened the valve, you had a "potential difference" between the two bottles. Now you have no potential difference. A piece of plain copper wire has no potential difference; connect it to a battery and you have a potential difference.

a force-attraction between the electrified particles concentrated at the positive and negative terminals. There is an electromotive force which exists between the two terminals. We call that force *potential difference* or, more commonly, *voltage*. Figure E-2

If we connect a wire to the two battery terminals, an electrical current will flow in the wire. We measure that flow in *amperes*. The number of amperes, or "amps," refers to the quantity of electrons passing a given point in one second. Figure E-3

In an electrical system, the conductor of electricity is usually a wire. When the electrical current runs through a wire, the wire creates a

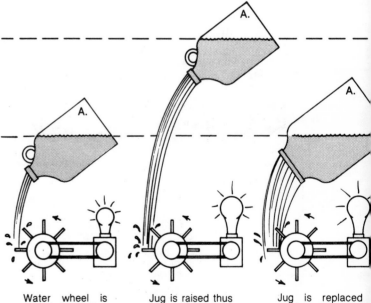

Water wheel is turned by falling water from Jug "A", lighting small bulb.

Jug is raised thus increasing potential lighting larger bulb.

Jug is replaced with larger mouthed jug increasing current and lighting larger bulb.

Figure E-3. **FALLING WATER ANALOGY DESCRIBING INCREASED POTENTIAL**

Figure E-4. **WATER PIPE SIZE ANALOGY OF ELECTRICAL RESISTANCE**

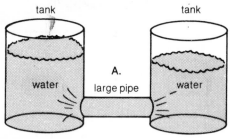

The water from the left tank in **A.** can reach the right tank through a large pipe. There is little resistance to the flow of water because the pipe is large.

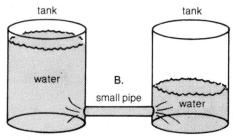

The pipe in **B.** is much thinner and smaller inside. It takes longer for the water to flow from one tank to another because the thin pipe offers more resistance to the flow of water.

Figure E-5. **WATER HOSE CONSTRICTION ANALOGY OF ELECTRICAL RESISTANCE**

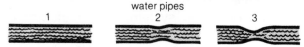

By squeezing the pipe resistance is increased.

Figure E-6. **WATER HOSE LENGTH ANALOGY OF ELECTRICAL RESISTANCE**

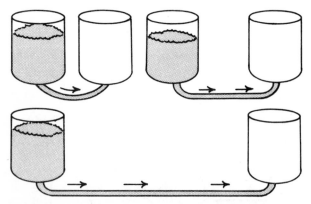

In the three sets of tanks above, the length of the hose connecting the tanks is another way to judge the resistance. The further the water must travel, the more resistance.

resistance to the current flow. To illustrate this, we can again use the analogy of water flow, as shown in Figures E-4, E-5, and E-6.

The *ohm* is the unit we use as a measure of electrical resistance. All substances resist, to a greater or lesser degree, the flow of electricity. Most metals are good conductors offering little resistance. On the other hand, rubber, wood, and glass are poor conductors offering high resistance, so we use these materials as insulators.

We can determine the amount of resistance in a conductor, or circuit, by dividing the voltage by the amps:

$$\frac{\text{volts}}{\text{amps}} = \text{ohms}$$

Let's say we have a circuit with a 200-volt potential and which has a 100 amp current. Using our formula, we find that the circuit is offering 2 ohms of resistance:

$$\frac{200 \text{ volts}}{100 \text{ amps}} = 2 \text{ ohms}$$

The higher the ohm rating, the more voltage is required to have a circuit with, in this case, a 100-amp flow.

The resistance to the flow of electricity in a light bulb filament is what causes the wire to burn brightly.

When we connected our two battery terminals with a wire to create a flow of electricity, we produced a source of power that we can harness to do work. We measure that power in *watts*. The combination of force, or voltage, and quantity of flow, or amps, creates watts, the unit of power. We express this in a simple formula:

$$\text{volts} \times \text{amps} = \text{watts}$$

If our positive and negative battery terminals have a potential difference of 5 volts between them, and we connect them into a circuit carrying 2 amps of current flow, we produce 10 watts of power:

$$5 \text{ volts} \times 2 \text{ amps} = 10 \text{ watts}$$

Some other units we use to describe electrical power are *horsepower* and *kilowatts*. These are related to watts, the basic power unit. One horsepower equals 746 watts. One kilowatt equals one thousand watts.

We use watts to do work for us—to light a bulb, turn a motor, or lift a weight. In households, electrical current is produced by utility generators. The more work you require electricity to do, the more wattage is consumed. Electric bills are usually stated in "kilowatt hours" of electricity used. A kilowatt hour is 1,000 watts (which is one kilowatt) used for one hour. If a light bulb uses 100 watts per hour, in ten hours it will have consumed one kilowatt hour of electricity. Or ten 100-watt bulbs burning for one hour each will also have consumed one kilowatt hour of electricity.

There are two types of electric current: alternating and direct. Direct current (DC) is the type of current produced by a battery. Direct current flows in one direction from its source. Alternating current (AC) fluctuates from positive to negative in a specific number of cycles per second. In the U.S. household current, which is AC, fluctuates at 60 hertz (or cycles per second), thereby producing 120 alternating pulses per second. Figure E-7

Figure E-7. AC CURRENT

AC current can be represented by a wave motion. We will discuss AC current later in the chapter on "motors."

THE MAGIC OF MAGNETISM

In ancient Greece, Socrates noted that a series of iron rings could support themselves, forming a chain, if held by a lodestone or "magnet." A natural magnet is a magnetic oxide of iron which attracts normal iron. The word meaning "magnet" was the name the Greeks gave the lodestone because of its discovery near Magnesia, in Thesaly.

A magnet has a north and south pole. When a magnet floats on a cork in water, it aligns itself with the north and south poles of the earth, because the earth is actually a large magnet.

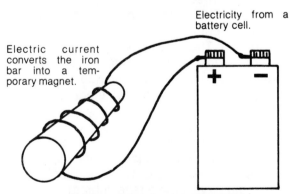

Electricity from a battery cell.

Electric current converts the iron bar into a temporary magnet.

Figure E-8. ELECTROMAGNETISM

When an electric current flows through wire wrapped around a bar of iron, an electromagnet is created. When the flow of electricity ceases, the magnetism ceases.

As early as 1000 A.D., the Chinese used magnets to create compasses, making use of the magnet's ability to point a needle north.

In 1820, Hans Christian Oersted discovered a relationship between magnetism and electric current. In an experiment, he noticed a compass needle move when placed next to a wire through which passed an electric current produced by a battery. Figure E-8. This observation was amplified by other scientists. From their experiments came electromagnetism, electric induction, electric generators and motors, plus a host of important milestones in science.

ELECTRIC INDUCTION

If the experiment shown in Figure E-9 had not worked, the world would be a vastly different place in which to live.

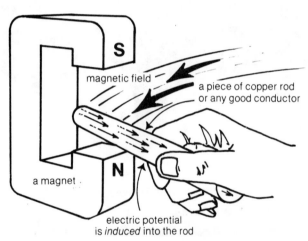

magnetic field

a piece of copper rod or any good conductor

a magnet

electric potential is *induced* into the rod

Figure E-9. ELECTRIC INDUCTION

When the metal rod is passed through the magnetic field, electricity is created by *induction*. The phenomenon above is the principle of the electric generator. That is, spinning a large conductor (rotor) within a magnetic field. Every time the rod passes through the magnetic field, electricity is "induced" into the rod.

Electric induction is, to my mind, one of the most important discoveries of science. Induction allowed the electrification of cities, and the use of motors in industry, transportation, farm mechanization, and much more.

We have looked briefly and simply at electricity and magnetism. Hopefully, this foundation of basic information will entice the more aggressive reader to research these subjects in greater depth. In any case, we now have enough information to proceed into the following chapters on motors, batteries, controls, and vehicles.

Electric Motors

Electric motors affect the life of virtually every person in the world. If an individual does not come into contact with electric clocks, trains, air conditioners, automobiles or any of the thousands of electric motor applications in his daily life, then he would have to be considered a primitive.

The similarity between a generator and a motor is that a generator converts mechanical energy into electrical energy, while an electric motor is a device that converts electrical energy into mechanical energy. The components of a DC motor and DC generator are almost identical. They both use or produce direct current. The discovery that a motor and a generator were interchangeable shook the nineteenth century with its brilliance.

This chapter is a sketch of electric motors and their application to electric vehicles. The avid reader interested in a more comprehensive explanation regarding some of the more exotic types .of AC induction and specialty motors is referred to the many textbooks and scientific data available on the subject.

The basis of all electric motors is a relationship between an electric current and magnetism. An electric current sets up a magnetic field at right angles to a wire carrying the current, as shown in Figure M-1.

**Figure M-1. MAGNETIC FIELD
PRODUCED BY ELECTRIC CURRENT**
A current sets up a magnetic field at right angles to a wire carrying the current.

If a compass is placed over a wire through which an electric current passes, the compass needle will be deflected. This discovery by Hans Christian Oersted in the early 19th century led to the application of electric induction, and the development of generators and electric motors.

The idea that like magnetic poles of magnets repulse each other, and unlike poles attract is the concept behind all electric motors. Electricity moves from the negative to the positive, through a wire, forming a circuit. The wire is now a miniature electromagnet. The positive side of the wire is the north pole and the negative side of the wire is the south pole. Like

poles will repel and unlike poles of north and south will attract. Figure M-2.

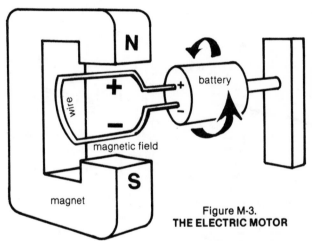

**Figure M-3.
THE ELECTRIC MOTOR**

An electric motor works because of induction. Basically, a motor is a generator working backwards. (The generator converts force into electricity by induction.) (The motor converts electricity into force through induction.)

Here's where the magic begins. Figure M-3.

As long as current runs through the wire loop, a miniature magnet will be formed, and the wire loop will turn *away* from the poles of the magnet. The positive side of the wire will not stay next to the north pole of the magnet. The

For this diagram let us suppose the small magnet is inside the large magnet's magnetic field. In this position, there is no motion because the opposite poles of each magnet attract each other.

But in this position, if we pretend we change the poles of the small magnet, the two magnets start to repulse each other. The small magnet must spin.

In this position, the opposite poles are pulling at each other and the small magnet must spin.

Figure M-2. ELECTROMAGNETISM IN MOTORS

negative side of the wire will move away from the south pole of the magnet causing the wire to twist. When the twisted wire's negative and positive sides are now matched to opposite poles of the magnet, the motion stops. The wire loop and the magnet are now at rest.

COMMUTATOR AND BRUSHES

An ingenious little device called a commutator allows the wire loop to continue flipping around and around.

Figure M-4 explains what the commutator does in basic terms, which is to keep the motor's armature (in this case our single wire loop) rotating in a continuous circle. The dark and light halves of the metal ring and its relationship to the two contacts, called brushes, show how this is accomplished.

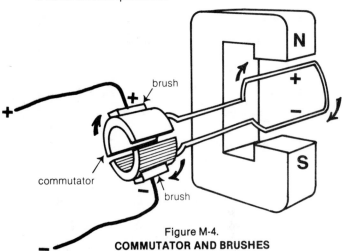

Figure M-4.
COMMUTATOR AND BRUSHES

As the wire loop spins from the repulsion of its magnetic force within the magnetic field of the larger magnet, the power from the battery is switched, through the contacts (brushes) from the light side to the dark side and back again to the light side and so on. In this way, the commutator insures that the (+) positive side of the wire loop is always in the position of repulsion by the north pole of the large magnet. Likewise, the (−) negative side is always in a continuous struggle against the force of the south pole of the large magnet.

As long as we apply a direct current, the loop will continue to spin in continuous motion, because of the commutator and brushes. Brushes can be made out of any good conductor, but generally they are made of carbon, in the form of graphite.

Our theoretical motor has one loop of wire

and a single split commutator. Actual motor construction may vary from a single heavy loop to thousands of wires wound around a soft iron armature, supported by bearings. Commutators in DC motors may have many contact points to effect a smooth transition of power through the brushes.

There are two basic types of motors, AC and DC. Earlier we mentioned that AC is alternating current, and that it moves back and forth in a wave of specific number of cycles. American household electrical current operates at 60 cycles per second.

Electric vehicles in use today generally use DC motors. The controls and other components are simpler in a DC system because battery and energy cells produce direct current. An AC motor must have the DC current converted to AC to be used in an electric vehicle. In DC motors, the basic types are series wound, shunt wound, compound, and permanent magnet.

PERMANENT MAGNET MOTOR

The permanent magnet motor is popular in many lightweight electric vehicle applications, such as bicycle power attachments and trolling motors for small boats. A permanent magnet is like a horseshoe magnet, which needs no electric current to produce magnetic flux. This highly efficient motor can use ceramic or metal magnets and sizes can vary from small motors for toys to larger multi-horsepower motors.

In the diagrams that showed one single loop of wire as a conductor, all used a permanent-type magnet for discussion purposes. We use electro-magnets which create a magnetic field by running electric current through a coil of wire.

THE SERIES MOTOR

The series wound, shunt wound and compound motors all use electro-magnetic field coils to produce a magnetic field. Most automotive starter motors are series wound. The series wound motor is popular in electric trucks, golf carts, winches, cranes and any application that requires high starting torque or "twisting" force. The useable torque and speed of the series motor varies under different load conditions. The heavier the load, the slower the motor speed; the lighter the load, the faster the motor speed. The dangerously high speeds possible under a no-load condition can ruin a series wound motor. Care must be taken to avoid this situation in an electric vehicle.

Figure M-5 is a diagram of a series motor:

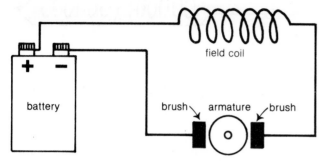

Figure M-5. SERIES MOTOR

In the series wound motor, the field coil is in "series" with the armature. The energy must go "through" the field coil before reaching the armature.

THE SHUNT MOTOR

The shunt motor utilizes a field coil in *parallel* with the armature. This means the current is supplied to both the field coil and the armature at the same time. The current does not have to go through the field coil to get to the armature. The low starting torque of the shunt motor does not lend itself to applications requiring full load start-ups. This motor is very popular for electric vehicle use.

Figure M-6 is a diagram of a shunt motor:

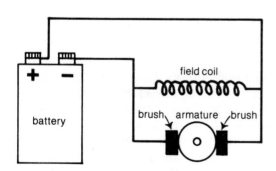

Figure M-6. SHUNT MOTOR

Notice how the field coil (electromagnet) and the armature receive current independent of each other.

THE COMPOUND MOTOR

A compromise between the series and shunt motor is the compound motor. Because it has two sets of field coils, conditions that would cause an absence of field excitation (which could burn out an ordinary shunt motor) do not exist.

The improved speed level, high starting torque, and capability of starting out in series and switching to shunt operation make the compound motor attractive in some applications. Elevators, and other heavy equipment uses are examples of compound motor application.

The compound, series, and shunt motors use direct current.

Figure M-7 is a diagram of the compound motor:

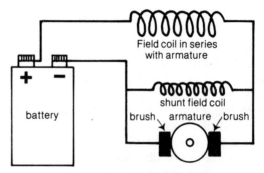

Figure M-7. COMPOUND MOTOR

Notice the two field coils. If a switch were provided to isolate the series field, there would be an even greater flexibility, allowing the unit to start out as a compound and run as a shunt motor.

AC MOTORS

Alternating current or AC motors are manufactured in more shapes, sizes, and for more applications than are DC motors. Household and industrial current produced by utility companies is alternating current; therefore, the majority of electric motors in use today are AC. *Most* AC motors do not need brushes or commutators, which makes them more economical to use and easier to maintain than direct current motors. AC motors have been used in electric cars and trucks by incorporating a device which converts the direct current of the batteries into alternating current.

Motors that will accept both AC and DC current are called "universal" motors.

For purposes of simplicity, we will not discuss all the various types of AC motors, because of their large number and their doubtful application to electric vehicles.

In the simple diagram of the DC motor, the commutator, with its split ring, made the wire loop switch up and back from positive to negative, so the wire loop flip-flopped around continuously when a current was provided.

Alternating current, on the other hand, provides an automatic way of flip-flopping current at a steady beat. Therefore, it is not necessary to do it mechanically with a commutator. The alternating current generators in power stations produce current at a steady alternating beat.

Power stations had many reasons to choose AC instead of DC. The simplicity of the AC generators allowed them to run without commutators and brushes which wear out. By running the AC generators (sometimes called alternators) at a constant regulated speed, a current that alternates at a dependable, steady 60 cycles or 120 flips per second could be maintained.

The first electric utility was the Pearl Street DC generating station in New York, built by Thomas Edison in 1882. As DC power stations proliferated, problems—such as power losses due to the length of the wires needed to reach any great distance—became evident. The lower voltages involved more power losses; the higher voltage possible with alternating current meant much lower power losses.

When AC generators, transformers, and the AC induction motor were perfected, power stations began switching to alternating current. A simple AC motor uses slip rings instead of a commutator to transfer a steady power to the wire loop. Figure M-8

Other AC motors use various forms of converting the alternating current impulses into mechanical force. The other forms are generally based on the use of a phenomenon known as mutual inductance.

An example of mutual inductance is shown in Figure M-9. When Coil B picks up the magnetic field of Coil A, a current is induced in the coil of wire B.

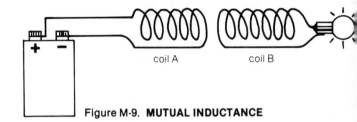

Figure M-9. **MUTUAL INDUCTANCE**

The induction motor was patented in the United States in 1888 by Nikola Tesla. Its basic principle is shown in Figure M-10. The compass needle always follows the bar magnet as it travels around the edge of the compass, because the south pole of the magnet attracts the north pole of the magnetized compass needle. The faster the magnet spins around, the faster the needle will spin.

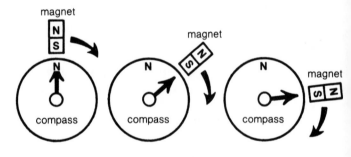

Figure M-10. **BASIC PRINCIPLE OF INDUCTION MOTOR**

Induction motors have two components. A stationary frame, called the "stator," that contains two or more sets of field coils, and a moveable center section called a "rotor."

The induction motor literally has a "rotating" magnetic field in the stator that reacts with the rotor in the same way our compass follows the magnet. If an induction motor has two poles in its stator and an alternating current of 60 Hertz (cycles per second) is applied, the motor would follow the rotating field at 60 revolutions per second. The speed at which the field rotates is referred to as its "synchronous" speed.

If the number of poles in the stator of an induction motor is increased, the synchronous speed will be slower. A two-pole, 60-hertz motor has a synchronous speed of 3,600 rpm, while a

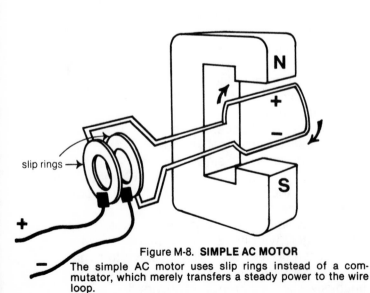

Figure M-8. **SIMPLE AC MOTOR**
The simple AC motor uses slip rings instead of a commutator, which merely transfers a steady power to the wire loop.

Figure M-11. **REVOLUTION OF A MAGNETIC FIELD IN INDUCTION MOTOR**

This diagram shows the rotating of a magnetic field in the stator of an induction motor with two sets of poles.

12-pole, 60-hertz motor has a synchronous speed of only 600 rpm.

The main advantage of the simple induction motor is that there is no physical connection between the stator and the rotor, and no electrical contact between the rotor and the power source (such as commutator and brushes on the DC motor). This saves money and time, since there is no need to replace brushes or clean the commutator.

The "mutual inductance" created as the rotating magnetic field of the stator cuts across the rotor's conductive windings, induces a voltage in the rotor's conductors. The interaction between the rotor current and the revolving magnetic field produces motor torque, which turns the rotor in the direction of the magnetic field.

Figure M-11 shows one revolution of a magnetic field in the stator of an induction motor which has two sets of poles.

The rotor of an induction motor never quite keeps up with the stator's revolving field. This is called the "slip," or the difference between the two speeds, and is responsible for the motor's torque. An induction motor whose rotor is in perfect step with the stator's rotating field is called a "synchronous" motor. The accuracy of electric clocks is testimony to the effectiveness of the synchronous motor.

LINEAR INDUCTION MOTORS

The linear AC motor is one in which the rotor and stator are laid out in a straight line rather than in a circle. When the power is turned "on" the motor produces a linear thrust instead of a rotary motion. If the vehicle or train can be supported by an air cushion or the force of magnetic repulsion, the need for wheels is totally eliminated. The basic purposes of the wheel is to convert rotary motion to linear motion and to support the vehicle above the ground. Eliminating the wheel and its attendant problems of noise, wheel-rail wear, and power loss in bearings, holds great potential value for future high speed mass transit systems. And the most attractive feature of the linear induction motor is that it has no moving parts.

There are two types of linear motors: the linear "induction" and the linear "synchronous." The underside of a linear induction vehicle is lined with electro-magnets facing each other, separated by a rail made of a non- magnetic metal. A magnetic wave is produced by the magnets which push against a "reaction rail" attached to the ground. The undulating magnetic wave motion causes an electric current to be "induced" into the reaction rail. This action pushes the vehicle forward by electro-magnetic force.

The linear synchronous motor uses the reaction of a large "on-board magnet" to push against the force induced into the electro-magnets buried in the ground under the vehicle. When the magnetic field of the track and the vehicle's magnet are in step with each other, they are "synchronous." A wave of magnetism in the track pushes against the magnetic field of the vehicle magnet, propelling the vehicle along like a wave carrying a leaf in water.

The motor system selected for a particular electric vehicle will obviously depend upon its use. A heavy duty van would use a different motor, control, and battery system than an electric three-wheel recreational vehicle. Expert engineers will design entire systems around the anticipated use of vehicles and incorporate AC or DC motors where suited.

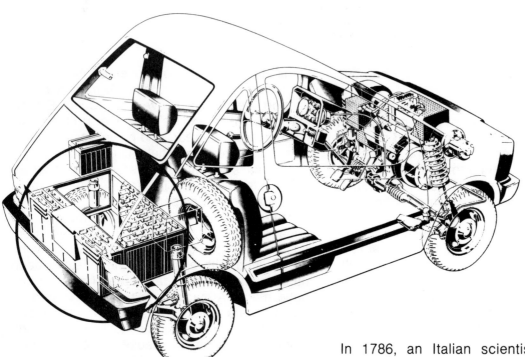

Batteries and Energy Systems

In 1786, an Italian scientist, Luigi Galvani, observed a relationship between electricity and chemistry which became the basis of the electro-chemical battery. During an experiment, he noticed a severed frog's leg twitch when touched to an iron rail and held by a copper hook. Electricity was produced by the interaction of the two metals within the flesh of the frog's leg, causing the muscles to contract.

The first battery was invented by an Italian scientist, Alessandro Volta, in about 1798. Volta's battery, called the "Voltaic pile," consisted of silver and zinc discs separated with cardboard soaked in salt water. A more efficient "primary" cell was conceived by an English chemist, John F. Daniell, in 1836. The first "secondary" battery, a lead-acid storage battery, was invented in 1859 by Gaston Planté, a French physicist.

The ancestor of the modern dry cell, the zinc-carbon cell, was invented by Georges Leclanche, a French scientist, in 1868. The term "Leclanche" is still used to describe this type of cell. For over one hundred years, many scientists have contributed to the steady development of cells and batteries.

In order to understand batteries, we must

first draw our attention to the simple cell, the building block of all batteries. Any "cell" consists of two dissimilar substances called electrodes, placed apart in a liquid called an "electrolyte." The electrolyte is a solution that acts upon the electrodes. It may be an acid, salt, or alkaline solution that will conduct electricity. Chemical action in the cell produces an electric current.

There are two types of cells: "primary" and "secondary." A primary cell is generally unrechargeable, while the secondary cell can be recharged.

PRIMARY CELLS

The flashlight battery is an example of a "primary" cell. The term "battery" in this case is misleading, because a battery is actually a combination of cells.

In the common carbon-zinc flashlight cell, there are three parts:

(1) An electrode of carbon which is placed in the center of (2) a moist paste electrolyte of ammonium chloride (made of water and a salt) contained by (3) a zinc case.

In figure B-1, the carbon rod is the positive electrode (anode) and the zinc case is the negative electrode (cathode).

Ions—electrically-charged atoms—pass from one electrode to another through the electrolyte. This process produces an electric current when the two electrodes are connected together in a circuit through a wire to a "load" such as a light bulb. The circuit is completed within the cell when ions flow in a current through the electrolyte solution.

For practical purposes, we will consider a simple carbon-zinc cell such as the flashlight

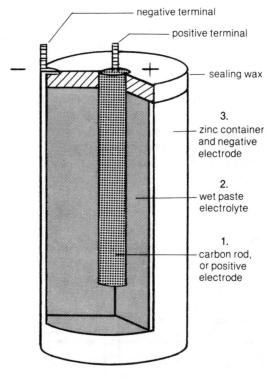

negative terminal
positive terminal
sealing wax

3.
zinc container and negative electrode

2.
wet paste electrolyte

1.
carbon rod, or positive electrode

Figure B-1. DRY CELL, CROSS-SECTIONAL VIEW

battery unrechargeable because when the electrolyte consumes the carbon or zinc electrode, chemical action ceases. The carbon-zinc cell, the oldest type of cell, produces about 1.5 volts of direct current, regardless of its size.

You can make your own primary cells in the experiments shown in Figure B-2.

Primary cells can be connected together to form a battery, which is a combination of cells. Figure B-3.

SECONDARY CELLS

The most unique characteristic of the secondary cell is that electric current can be used to

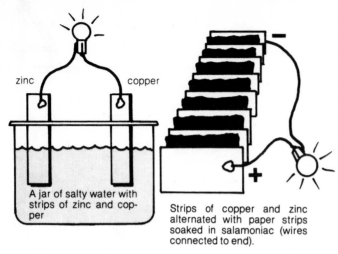

zinc

copper

A jar of salty water with strips of zinc and copper

Strips of copper and zinc alternated with paper strips soaked in salamoniac (wires connected to end).

Figure B-2. PRIMARY CELLS

"reverse" the chemical conditions within the cell, and replenish the chemical properties of the electrodes and electrolyte. Therefore, the cell can be used over and over again in discharging and recharging cycles. Secondary cells are used in combinations to form storage batteries, which produce electric current by chemical action.

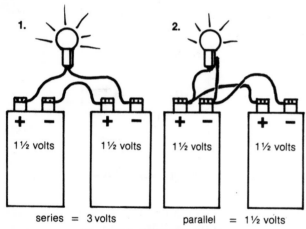

1.

2.

+ − 1½ volts

+ − 1½ volts

+ − 1½ volts

+ − 1½ volts

series = 3 volts

parallel = 1½ volts

Figure B-3. PRIMARY CELLS CONNECTED TO FORM BATTERY

When cells are connected together they form larger batteries in two ways.

THE LEAD-ACID BATTERY

The most popular storage battery of all time consists of lead-acid cells.

Gaston Plante' developed the rechargeable secondary cell in about 1859. This was the ancestor of the lead-acid battery. Storage batteries became popular in the wake of the Edison electric generating stations, around 1875. Un-

fortunately, the inefficient early lead-acid batteries had to be replaced after a few months of service.

The lead-acid storage battery consists of several identical cells containing two types of lead plates immersed in an electrolyte of sulfuric acid and water. Each cell has two electrodes with positive and negative plates. The positive plates are made of lead dioxide, the negative plates are sponge lead. (See battery cut-a-way view.)

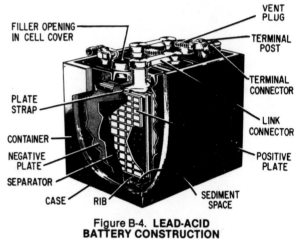

FILLER OPENING IN CELL COVER

VENT PLUG

TERMINAL POST

TERMINAL CONNECTOR

PLATE STRAP

LINK CONNECTOR

CONTAINER

NEGATIVE PLATE

POSITIVE PLATE

SEPARATOR

CASE

RIB

SEDIMENT SPACE

Figure B-4. LEAD-ACID BATTERY CONSTRUCTION

All positive and negative plates are insulated by separators made of a non-conductive material such as plastic. Each fully charged cell produces approximately 2 volts. Thus, a 6-volt battery has 3 cells, while a 12-volt battery has 6 cells. The cells are housed in a hard rubber or plastic container called a "battery case." The specific gravity of the electrolyte in a lead-acid battery is used to determine the state of charge of the cells. A fully charged cell has a specific gravity of about 1.30 and a voltage reading of 2 volts.

Specific gravity is used to measure the strength or percentage of sulfuric acid present in the electrolyte. If the specific gravity of a cell in a charged battery is 1.275, the electrolyte is 1.275 times as dense as water. Specific gravity is measured by a device called a hydrometer, which consists of a float in a glass tube.

HOW A LEAD-ACID BATTERY WORKS:

Figure B-5, (Illustration #1), shows one cell of a fully charged lead-acid battery. The specific gravity of the electrolyte is 1.275.

The negative plate is sponge lead. The positive plate is lead peroxide. The electrolyte is maximum sulfuric acid with a minimum percentage of water. As we start to discharge the cell (Illustration #2) by attaching a light bulb, the following chemical processes begin:

The ions (electrically-charged atoms) of one electrode pass to the other electrode through the electrolyte and change the composition of the metal electrodes and the electrolyte.

When the cell is fully discharged (Illustration #3), the electrolyte contains a minimum of sulfuric acid and a maximum of water. The specific gravity of the electrolyte is now about 1.110 (or 1.11 times the density of water.)

In the totally discharged cell, the plates cannot produce current because they are both covered with lead sulfate and the electrolyte is weak. The electrolyte is predominantly water instead of sulfuric acid. When we connect the cell to a battery charger, (Illustration #4), the action reverses itself.

This action continues until the cell is fully charged.

Before further discussing the new energy systems, we must define our terminology and methods of rating. To do this, we must turn to the lead-acid battery for examples of each term.

BATTERY CAPACITY

The term "ampere hours" refers to the number of amperes a battery is capable of producing in a circuit for a given number of hours. A lead-acid battery that is rated at 80-ampere-hours capacity is one that can, for example:

Maintain 20 amperes for 4 hours

or

10 amperes for 8 hours

When temperatures drop, the lead-acid battery loses capacity. At 0°F, (−18°C), a battery has lost 60% of its power. So a lead-acid battery called upon to start an automobile in cold weather will have less capacity than in warm weather. Also, the car's engine oil, becomes thicker in the cold, further increasing the starting power needs.

Another type of battery rating is "cold-cranking amps." This rating shows the ability of the battery to produce high energy for a brief period, at maximum output. For example, a 95 amp hour battery, such as used in a large automobile, may have 515 cold-cranking amps at 0°F. (−18°C) for 30 seconds.

A relatively new method of rating lead-acid

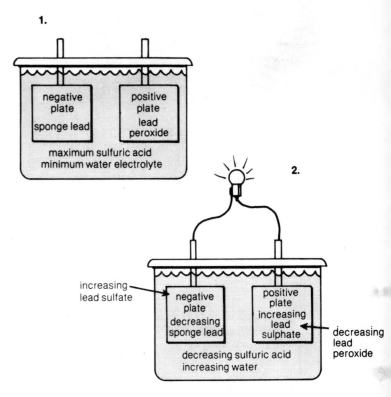

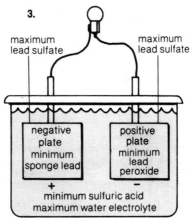

In the totally discharged cell, the plates can no longer yield useable chemical activity to produce current. Water is predominent in the electrolyte instead of sulphuric acid.

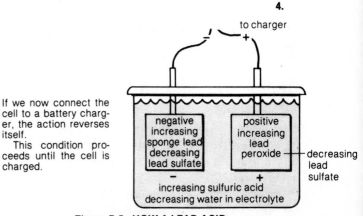

If we now connect the cell to a battery charger, the action reverses itself.

This condition proceeds until the cell is charged.

Figure B-5. HOW A LEAD-ACID BATTERY WORKS

batteries is the number of minutes a fully charged battery can produce current at a 25 amp discharge rate at 80°F. (27°C). This usually ranges from 50 to 150 minutes, depending on the size or number of plates in the battery.

ENERGY DENSITY

The amount of power a battery can produce for a certain length of time relative to its own weight is called "energy density," or "specific energy". This is expressed in watt-hours per pound (per kg.) of battery weight, or abbreviated as w-hr/lb. (w-hr/kg.). A lead-acid battery is generally rated at 8 to 12 w-hr/lb, (17.6 to 26.4 wh/kg) and can deliver up to 16 to 20 w-hr/lb (35 to 44 wh/kg) under low current-drain conditions.

IMPORTANT NOTE:

Throughout this book, we will compare alternate battery systems to the lead-acid battery as a point of reference. If a new system can produce a 40 wh/lb (88 wh/kg) energy density, for example, we compare it to the 20 wh/lb (44 wh/kg) maximum rating of the lead-acid battery to note an energy storage "twice" as great as the lead-acid type. This means a vehicle can carry half the new batteries to equal an identical range of the lead-acid battery.

POWER DENSITY

Another commonly used term is "power density", expressed in "watts per pound" of battery weight. This is the power available at any one time, under optimum conditions. This peak output is important for acceleration and top speed. A lead-acid battery under prime conditions for a brief period may approach 35 w/lb (77 w/kg) output.

OPERATING CYCLES

An "operating cycle" refers to one complete discharge cycle of a particular battery system. In an electric car, it would be the number of times the fully charged battery system could be totally drained of energy. Under normal use, everyday electric vehicle driving would not completely drain or "deep cycle" the batteries. However, this rating is a guide to the maximum number of total discharges of a battery in theoretical use. A lead-acid battery is rated at about 400 deep cycles.

COST

Another important consideration for any battery system to prove worthy of electric vehicle duty is the cost factor. We will use the term "dollars per kilowatt hour" as a guide to the cost of an energy system. This is expressed as $/kwh.

Today's lead-acid batteries have a cost factor of $50/kwh. A battery proposed by Exxon Enterprises, Inc., utilizes a lithium-titanium-disulfide system. Costs are projected at $35/kwh for a mass-produced version.

THE LEAD ACID BATTERY

In electric vehicles, combinations of batteries are used to achieve desired voltages. They are connected together in series or parallel, depending upon the voltage needed.

The design of the lead-acid battery is determined by several factors including the number of plates per cell and the amount of active material per cell. Some batteries have thin plates which provide high specific power because of their lower electrical resistance. Other battery designs use thicker plates which give them a high cycle life because they have a large amount of active material. The active material in each cell determines the specific energy and the total energy.

There are four types of lead-acid batteries in use. The SLI battery (starting, lighting, and ignition), the golf cart battery, the semi-industrial battery, and the industrial battery.

The SLI battery can deliver high power output for a short period of time and at varying temperatures. This type of battery is used to start internal combustion vehicles such as the automobile. The energy available from an SLI battery is less than that of a golf cart battery because the SLI has thin plates which are lightly loaded with active material. The use of thin plates allows high specific power, but also results in short deep-cycle discharge life. Generally speaking, an SLI battery in an automobile is limited to less than 100 deep-discharge cycles but, because the type of discharge normally associated with automobiles is very light (usually only 10%), the life of the SLI battery may exceed 1,000 cycles.

Photo courtesy of S.G.L.
Batteries Mfg., Detroit, Mich.

A "DEEP CYCLE" GOLF CART BATTERY DESIGNED FOR ELECTRIC VEHICLE DUTY.

The golf cart battery must be capable of supplying a relatively high power output for long periods of time, while maintaining low battery weight. Battery manufacturers have improved golf cart battery performance to make them more compatible with electric vehicle needs. The golf cart battery has thicker plates than the SLI battery and is designed for a deep-discharge cycle life in the 200 to 400 cycle range. The golf cart battery is used in some small vehicles, such as cars and vans, because of its convenient size and accessibility. Golf cart batteries weigh in about 60 to 70 pounds (27 to 32 kg).

Semi-industrial battery requirements lie between the golf cart and the industrial battery. The semi-industrial battery has a higher specific energy than the industrial battery, yet can deliver energy for a longer period of time than a golf cart battery. The thicker plates yield a high cycle life, yet they are thin enough to maintain high specific energies. The deep-discharge cycle life of the semi-industrial battery can range from 500 to 1,000 cycles.

Industrial batteries are used mainly as a power source for lift trucks, where cycle life and total available energy are important. Industrial batteries may use tubular positive plates instead of the standard pasted plates. Tubular industrial batteries have exhibited long deep-discharge cycle lives of 1,000 to 2,000 cycles. They have a high resistance to abuse, but cannot attain the power density of the golf cart or semi-industrial battery.

The cost of lead-acid batteries depends upon the type. The SLI battery has an initial cost of $68/kwh, the golf cart battery has an initial cost of $50/kwh, the semi-industrial battery has an initial cost of $210/kwh, and the industrial battery is even more expensive. While the SLI battery may seem less expensive per kilowatt hour of initial cost than the industrial, one must remember that after cycle life has been computed, the SLI battery costs more per cycle, compared to the industrial battery.

Considerations for electric vehicle use determine the type of battery to be used. The industrial battery may be too heavy for a vehicle, and not be capable of maintaining the specific power necessary to push the vehicle up to high speed. Yet its cycle life is very attractive. Also, remember that the type of driving to which an electric vehicle is subjected determines both the range per charge as well as the total cycle life of the battery. High speeds and rapid acceleration will dramatically reduce the effective

Photo courtesy of Lead Industries Association

A truckload of scrapped lead from batteries is hoisted aloft by a hydraulic mechanism that dumps the lead into an outdoor storage area to await processing into recycled lead.

Lead scrap is unique in that most of it comes from batteries, which require more lead than any other end-use application of the metal. For example, in 1973, the battery industry consumed nearly 770,000 tons of lead. Of that total, 645,000 tons were recovered from various forms of scrap, and about 63 per cent of that total came from scrapped batteries.

range per charge of a vehicle. The distance the vehicle will travel decreases as the number of accelerations per charge increases.

The total amount of energy that can be removed from a lead-acid battery depends upon the rate at which the energy is withdrawn. Today's lead-acid battery can only deliver 40% of its capacity if discharged in a 20 minute period, compared to 100% delivery in a one-hour discharge period. Therefore, an electric vehicle travelling at high speeds would deplete its batteries much faster than it would if it were driving at moderate speeds.

The temperature of the electrolyte in a lead-acid battery and the age of the battery can affect the amount of available energy. When the battery is subjected to low temperatures, the electrolyte becomes more resistant to current flow. The age of a battery affects its performance. A new battery actually will begin to increase its capacity about the first 10 to 20% of its life. Then the energy density peaks and begins to decline. Another factor that determines the longevity of a battery is the type of service to which it is subjected. In cases of deep discharges, the life of the battery is reduced significantly. Therefore, an electric vehicle driven to the point of running out of power will have a lesser number of cycles left in the battery than a comparable vehicle which is driven to only 80% of its discharge depth.

Battery care is the most important consideration for an electric vehicle. It is in this area that most weaknesses of an electric vehicle will be found. The state of charge and the maintenance of ample water levels in batteries is most important. Attending to corrosion on terminal posts and checking to make sure connections are secure should be considered a routine procedure, because lead-acid batteries are vulnerable to an effect called "sulfating," the formation of sulfate deposits around the plates. This can result in the destruction of the cell.

While interim and advanced technology battery systems have other problem areas, sulfating remains the plague of most lead-acid batteries. One solution to help avoid the effects of sulfating is to keep a battery at the highest charge level possible at all times, without overcharging. The wise user of an electric vehicle charges the batteries fully before starting a trip. It is unwise to let a vehicle stand for long periods of time without attaching a battery charger to maintain a full charge when the vehicle is not in use.

Because maintenance will determine a battery's useful life, care must be taken to avoid overcharging, which is not only wasteful of energy and economically undesirable, it shortens the battery life. Generally speaking, both overcharging *and* undercharging reduce the life of a battery. Undercharging reduces the total energy available so that damage may result due to deep cycling. Also, the simple procedure of a regularly-scheduled topping off of the electrolyte with water as a routine procedure can extend battery life significantly.

ELECTRIC VEHICLE BATTERIES

In the near future, batteries used in electric vehicles will probably be of the lead-acid variety. Even though patents for the lead-sulfuric acid secondary cell ran out around the turn of the century, a million batteries of this type are sold annually for electric golf carts alone. Electric forklifts, automobiles, delivery vans, and other commercial applications significantly increase the number of lead-acid batteries in use.

In order to survive, electric vehicle batteries of the future will have to be lighter, more powerful, durable, economical, and have longer lives. Therefore, the battery of the future will have to be a "superbattery."

The list of potential substitutes for the lead-acid battery is impressive. It would take a volume easily as large as this book to delve into the technical characteristics of each of these potential energy systems.

For those who wish to research this subject more intensely, here are the alternatives: batteries using nickel-iron, nickel-cadmium, silver-zinc, silver-cadmium, lithium-chlorine, sodium-sulfur, zinc-chlorine, lithium-iron-sulfide, zinc-nickel oxide, zinc-air, nickel-zinc, lithium-titanium sulfide, lithium-sulfur, aluminum-chlorine, iron-lithium, lithium-water, and hydrogen-oxygen materials, as well as monopolar, lithium-unipolar, and lead-cobalt-tripolar systems, to name but a few.

Out of this list, we will discuss six systems, because they are advanced to the point where construction and operation of a working battery for a vehicle is possible. These candidates are: nickel-zinc, nickel-iron, zinc-air, iron-air, zinc-chlorine hydrate, and sodium-sulfur.

THE NICKEL-ZINC BATTERY

The zinc-nickel oxide battery was patented by a

Photo courtesy of
Yardney Electric Corporation

YARDNEY NICKEL-ZINC BATTERIES

The Yardney Electric Company of Pawcatuck, Connecticut, U.S.A., has been associated with nickel-zinc batteries since the mid-1960's. Yardney has demonstrated that nickel-zinc can double the range of on-road electric test vehicles over lead-acid batteries. One demonstration used a Sebring-Vanguard Citicar equipped with nickel-zinc batteries. Another used the Fiat X1/23 Electric City Car. The 300 AH 6.4-V battery module shown can provide 2-1/2 times the stored energy of a lead-acid traction battery with the same size and volume.

MODEL OF A 300AH, 6.4 VOLT NICKEL ZINC BATTERY MODULE
This module would provide 2-1/2 times the stored energy of a lead-acid traction battery of the same weight and volume.

Photo courtesy of Yardney Electric Corporation

Russian inventor in 1901, but problems such as short life, low performance, and high cost have limited interest in this system.

Progress by companies such as General Motors has helped bring some of the problems under control. A GM process reduces the amount of nickel required, thus lowering cost and weight of cells. Remember, zinc is used very effectively in primary cells; the problems have always been related to recharging. Today, the advantages of the nickel-zinc battery make it a potential candidate to replace the lead-acid battery in electric vehicles. Theoretically, the range of an electric vehicle may be more than doubled by using nickel-zinc over lead-acid batteries.

In tests conducted by N.A.S.A. on a ¼-ton van powered by nickel-zinc batteries, there was an improvement of 87% in range over golf car

lead-acid batteries. At 20-mph (32 km/hr), the nickel-zinc version travelled 54.9 miles (88.3 km), and the golf cart battery version travelled 29.4 miles (47.3 km). Compared to a semi-industrial lead-acid battery in one test, the nickel-zinc showed 75% improvement in a stop-and-go driving cycle.

During another test, an electric automobile, at a 40-mph (64 km/hr) speed, demonstrated an 82% range improvement over golf cart batteries, travelling 146 miles (235 km) with the nickel-zinc batteries compared to 80 miles (129 km) with lead-acid golf cart batteries.

The cell of the nickel-zinc battery, in a discharged state, consists of aqueous potassium hydroxide (KOH) as an electrolyte. A medium-sized cell of 145 amp hours exhibited a life of over 1,000 cycles by vibrating the zinc electrode. Vibration prevented zinc-dendrites

EAGLE PICHER NICKEL-ZINC POWERED VEHICLE

The Eagle Picher Company of Joplin, Missouri, U.S.A., has produced a prototype electric recreational vehicle using nickel-zinc battery technology.

The 965-lb (439-kg) two-seater carries 375 lbs (170 kg) of batteries and has a cruise speed of 25 mph (40 km/hr) and a range of 65 miles per charge using a 2-hp motor.

Photo courtesy of Eagle Picher

from forming. Zinc-dendrite formations, which are needle-like zinc structures, have been a problem with this type of cell because they penetrate the separators and short out the cell.

Because no large-scale production of the nickel-zinc battery presently exists, costs are prohibitive. However, costs of $50/kwh are projected. Several sources indicate the possibility of a nickel-zinc system being commercially available by 1980.

THE NICKEL-IRON BATTERY

Thomas Edison had developed a battery for the electric vehicles of his day known as the ''Edison Cell,'' which was a nickel-iron storage battery. This battery was used extensively in early electric cars. Patents for the ''Edison Cell'' ran out before the First World War, but some vehicles continued to use them thereafter with remarkable longevity. Because the Edison cell produces only 1.2 volts, a ten-cell battery is needed to equal 12 volts. This system may well yet be a contender for the next generation of electric vehicle batteries.

The nickel-iron battery has a life of over 1,000 cycles and reported power density of 45 w/lb (99 w/kg) and specific energy of 20 w-hr/lb

(44 w-hr/kg) at a 2-hour rate. Costs of $50 to $120 per/kwh are projected for this battery. Actual price estimates for nickel-zinc and nickel-iron systems are difficult to estimate because of variable mass production costs. A point in favor or these systems is the possibility of reclaiming the nickel.

One Japanese study reported a nickel-iron performance of 38 w-hr/lb (84 w-hr/kg) at the 5 to 7-hour rate of discharge and a life of 500 cycles.

A nickel-iron system has been installed and tested in two electric vehicles by Westinghouse. One was a van and the other an automobile. The nickel-iron system demonstrated a 50% improvement in the range of both vehicles over the range of golf cart lead-acid batteries.

The nickel-iron battery system is not efficient during recharging, compared with a lead-acid battery. When charging, the nickel-iron battery stores only 50 to 60% of the current compared with 75% efficiency for the lead-acid battery.

When charging, the nickel-iron battery gives off more hydrogen than a similar lead-acid battery. This causes loss of water from the electrolyte. Therefore, charging not only requires cooling for the system, but care must be taken that hydrogen is properly vented to avoid combustion.

METAL-AIR BATTERIES

The two metal-air batteries considered for longer term future use are the iron-air and zinc-air variety. Tests from foreign sources indicate 300 to 400% improvement in specific energy ratings over lead-acid systems. Cycle life is reported to be about 300 cycles and energy densities from 38 to 55 w-hr/lb (84 to 121 w-hr/kg).

The metal-air systems have a relatively high specific energy level and are lightweight because air reacts directly with the metals, but they are limited in peak power output. Therefore, they are being used in electro-chemical hybrid-battery systems for vehicles. Hybrid batteries incorporate the high specific energy of one battery system with a second battery system designed to produce high peak power. In operation, the high specific energy battery—that is, the zinc-air or iron-air—provides the energy necessary for cruising. When the need for acceleration or passing is required, the load is transfered to a high current battery, which is connected into the system. A relatively small high current battery, such as a lead-acid type, can meet the peak demand that is needed and can be recharged from the energy of the battery pack when acceleration is not required.

Both zinc-air and iron-air batteries were combined with high power lead-acid batteries in hybrid configurations in tests made in Japan. The Daihatsu Lightweight Passenger Automobile powered by an iron-air/lead-acid hybrid system travelled 162 miles (260 km) at 25 mph (40 km/hr). Two other vehicles, one automobile and one truck, with hybrid zinc-air/lead-acid batteries had ranges of 283 miles and 308 miles (455 and 496 km) respectively, at the same speed.

ZINC-CHLORINE HYDRATE BATTERY

The high specific energy possible with the electro-chemical coupling of chlorine and zinc makes this type of battery system very attractive. The problem with this system is the need for a safe and practical method of storing chlorine. A zinc-chlorine hydrate battery was developed by Energy Development Associates (EDA) which solved the problem by storing chlorine as a solid hydrate (hydrogen compound). The storage temperatures are about 46 degrees F (8 degrees C) and the system uses pumps, filters, and a refrigeration unit. This system has demonstrated specific energy of 30 w-hr/lb (66 w- hr/kg) and has a projected specific energy of 75 w-hr/lb (165 w-hr/kg) for vehicle use. In a test made using a converted EDA Vega, the zinc- chlorine hydrate battery

COMPARISON OF THREE BATTERY TECHNOLOGIES
The three battery cells shown here have the same energy storage capacity. At left is a conventional lead-acid battery. The next two are experimental batteries under development at General Motors Research Laboratories, Warren, Mich. In the center is the zinc/nickel oxide battery, about 1/3 the size and weight of the lead-acid; at right is the lithium/iron sulfide, about 1/6 the size and weight.

reported a range of 150 miles (240 km) at 50 mph (80 km/hr).

EDA predicts an urban 4-passenger vehicle could have a 150-200 mile range at 50 mph (80 km/hr) and a 75 mph (121 km/hr) top speed. The battery life would be 100,000 miles with a possible $30/kwh in a developed market.

HIGH TEMPERATURE BATTERIES

For electric vehicle use, the sodium-sulfur battery lies in the more distant future. This high temperature system could make it possible for a vehicle to travel 200 miles (320 km) on one charge. Laboratory tests using single cells have approached specific energy of 45 w-hr/lb (99 w-hr/kg). This is almost four times the energy density of a lead-acid battery. In this system the sodium and sulfur must be in liquid form, which requires an operating temperature of 570 degrees to 750 degrees F (300 degrees to 400 degrees C). The electrolyte is solid and made of ceramic or glass-fiber material.

A prototype vehicle using a sodium-sulfur battery was tested in 1973 by the Electric Council in England. The electric van was capable of travelling more than 100 miles (160 km) on a single charge.

Another sodium-sulfur battery is being developed by the Ford Motor Co. which uses molten sodium and sulfur electrodes. The electrolyte is a solid ceramic, beta-alumina. The battery was tested by Ford in an automobile that attained a speed of 70 miles per hour (113 km).

Problems associated with this cell will have to be worked out, including charging procedures, high temperature seals, and electrolyte considerations.

Both sodium and sulfur are cheap and abundant materials. When operating and manufacturing problems are solved, this will be an excellent system. Other batteries in the "molten salt" family include lithium-sulfur and lithium-chlorine.

A lithium/iron sulfide battery cell was tested by General Motors. The experimental cell operated for over 10,000 hours. This molten salt battery operates in the range of 650 to 900F (350 to 480C). The cell can hold as much energy as five to ten lead-acid cells. Tests yielded ratings of 700 deep discharge cycles during 14 months of continuous operation. GM designers believe that the lithium/iron sulfide battery could increase the range of a lead-acid powered com-

muter vehicle from 30 to 200 miles (48 to 320 km) per charge. This cell is strictly experimental at this time, with production expectations relegated to the far distant future.

FUEL CELLS

The fuel cell, invented by Grove in 1839, was designed to electrolyze water with electrical energy from a hydrogen-oxygen battery.

Recently, there has been great interest in the concept of the fuel cell for vehicle use. This renewed interest began with fuel cell innovations used in the space program. The NASA Gemini program was the first practical use of a fuel cell; General Electric designed the Gemini fuel cell.

The Gemini system did not use an aqueous (liquid) electrolyte. Instead it used a special polymer membrane, much like a sponge, which eliminated certain electrolyte container problems. This special type of hydrogen oxygen cell used platinum in the electrodes and may not be practical for electric vehicles on earth. Although their excellent power-to-weight-and-size ratio make them ideal for electric vehicle use, they are far too costly.

A fuel cell produces electricity by utilizing a fuel and an oxidizer. The fuel can be kerosene or another hydrocarbon such as natural gas, methanol, or even gasoline. The fuel is combined with an oxidizer such as air or oxygen slowly in a controlled manner to produce electric current when a catalyst is added. (A catalyst is something that causes a chemical reaction without being itself consumed in the process.) Platinum, silver, or nickel are examples of catalysts used in fuel cells. Although fuel cells are subject to some heat loss, they have efficiencies of 84% at room or "ambient" temperatures.

By far the most popular fuel cell is the hydrogen-air and hydrogen-oxygen type which is being developed in a number of countries by many companies using various combinations of catalysts, electrodes and electrolytes. The hydrogen-oxygen cell produces emissions that do not cause pollution because combining hydrogen and oxygen results in the formation of pure water.

Because hydrogen and oxygen in combination are used as rocket fuel, storage is a sensitive area. Care must be taken to avoid sparks that could cause an explosion. The use of pressurized tanks or super-cooled (cryogenically) stored liquid hydrogen and oxygen suggest two storage possibilities.

Another method for storing hydrogen is called the metal-hydride system. This system is accomplished by pumping hydrogen into specially designed tanks that contain metal hydrides (such as a combination of iron and titanium alloy) into which hydrogen is absorbed. The difficulties of cryogenic storage, which requires complicated hardware to lower the temperature sufficiently to liquify hydrogen, are overcome to an extent with the hydride system. The advantages of ambient temperatures and the lack of high pressure and safer storage, make the hydride system attractive. Because hydride storage can absorb hydrogen about 75% as well as cryogenic methods, this type of system will probably be used extensively in the future.

Virtually all internal-combustion-powered vehicles can be converted to burn hydrogen-air or hydrogen-oxygen mixtures. Experimental automobiles have been built using this concept. There is a strong probability that we will see hydrogen used in some form in the vehicles of tomorrow. Perhaps the future use of the fuel cell (and of hydrogen in general) will be oriented to large utility companies that produce electric power. The advantages of the fuel cell for mass electrical production will probably be associated with the excess energy from nuclear generating stations. These stations must operate at high capacity in order to retain efficiencies. Also, there is a lower demand for electric power during off hours, when electric consumption is moderate. By producing hydrogen through electrolysis during these off-peak hours, the energy normally wasted could be stored as hydrogen to be used later as required in fuel cells or sold directly to natural gas companies.

CONCLUSION

While the lead-acid battery represents the state of the art for electric vehicle batteries of today, work is being done in many countries to improve its performance and life. The lead-acid batteries of today can provide enough range in advanced vehicle designs to fill many of the functions necessary for an electric vehicle.

Argonne National Laboratory made a study to determine the acceptable range of an electric passenger automobile. The study showed that

COMPACT BATTERY CELL
Under development at General Motors Research Laboratories is the "lithium/iron sulfide" battery, a high performance battery that may someday greatly extend the range of electric vehicles—to 200 miles or more between recharges.

Here, GM senior research engineer Thompson G. Bradley works on an experimental battery cell housed in a nonreactive helium atmosphere. The battery is cooled down from its normal operating temperature of 870 °F, about that found in a home "self-cleaning" oven.

an 88-mile-per-day range would meet most of the needs of the U.S. driver. In order to accomplish this, a vehicle battery system would require an energy density of about 30 to 50 w-hr/lb (66 to 110 w-hr/kg) and a capacity of 20 to 25 kwh at a cost of about $30/kwh. Today's lead-acid batteries have energy densities of about 10 to 14 w-hr/lb (22 to 31 w-hr/kg). The range of the lead-acid powered vehicle is about 25 to 40 miles (40 to 64 km) per charge with the cost for current lead-acid batteries in the $50 to $70/kwh range. Reports from battery manufacturers indicate possible energy densities of advance lead-acid designs of 20 to 25 w-hr/lb (44 to 55 w-hr/kg) in the near future. Also, a number of improvements can be made to reduce weight without power reduction.

All of the new battery systems that are under

consideration have specific energies which are higher than those of lead-acid batteries. But problems involving limited life, charging difficulties, complexity of systems, and high costs have prevented their use in vehicles. Although they are presently under development and available at great cost it may be three to five years before we see the nickel-zinc battery in production at a cost competitive with the lead-acid battery. Other batteries will be adopted as their technologies progress in the distant future.

We have discussed some of the various battery approaches to power storage for an electric vehicle. Perhaps hybrids of more than one type of battery may eventually be used in a single vehicle. Certainly, the advantages of the long life nickel-iron and the power density of an advanced lead-acid battery could be combined in a way that would utilize the strengths of each system. The new system that can stand the test of practical daily use, ease of operation, and marketing acceptability will obviously be the winner.

Development Goals For Near Term Electric Vehicle Batteries*

Calendar Year	Lead-Acid			Nickel/Iron			Nickel/Zinc		
	1977	1978	1980	1977	1978	1980	1977	1978	1980
Specific Energy (watt-hours/kilogram)	30	40	50	44	50	60	70	70	90
Specific Power (watts/kilogram) Sustaining	15	20	25	20	40	50	20	40	50
Peak	50	100	150	130	150	200	130	150	200
Energy Efficiency (%)	65	>60	>60	70	70	70	>60	>60	60
Cycle Life	700	800	1000	1500	1500	2000	200	500	700
Initial Installed Cost ($/kilowatt-hour) for less than 10,000 batteries	100	80-100	80-100		100-120	100-120		100-120	100-120
for more than 10,000 batteries	50	50	40	120	70-80	50-60		70-80	50-60

* Batteries Duty Cycle: 2-4 hr Discharge, 70-80% Depth of Discharge 1-6 hr. Charge

Potential Electric Vehicle Batteries

Systems	Electrolytes	Temp.°C	Current				Projected			
			Watt-Hours/Kilogram	Watts/Kilogram (Peak)	Life (Cycles)	Cost $/KWH	Watt-Hours/Kilogram	Watts/Kilogram (Peak)	Life (Cycles)	Cost $/KWH
Near-Term (1-2 yr)										
Lead-Acid (SOA)	Sulfuric Acid	Room Ambient	30	50	700	50	50	150	>1000	50
Nickel-Iron	Potassium Hydroxide	Room Ambient	44	130	1500	120	60	150	>1000	120
Intermediate Term (3-5 yr)										
Lead-Acid (Advanced)	Sulfuric Acid	Room Ambient	—	—		—	50	150	>1000	60
Nickel-Zinc	Potassium Hydroxide	Room Ambient	70	110	200	800	90	150	>1000	50
Long-Term (5 yr)										
Zinc/Iron-Air	Potassium Hydroxide	Room Ambient	80-120	40	150	2000	90	80	>1000	60
Zinc-Chlorine	Zinc Chlorine	Room Ambient	66	60	100	2000	130	150	>1000	50
Lithium-Metal Sulfide	Lithium/Potassium Chloride	400-450	100	120	250	2000	150	300	>1000	40
Sodium-Sulfur	Beta-Alumina	300-350	90	100	200	2000	170	200	>1000	40

Electric Vehicle Controls

All vehicles require some form of control system. We are all conversant with the controls of a conventional automobile, which include the accelerator, brake, shifting mechanism, and steering. The motorized cranes used in construction have a great number of controls to perform a variety of complicated duties. Electric vehicles need controls that will extract the most power and range from an energy system.

Historically, electric cars contained controllers that would isolate various segments of a battery pack. Electric cars such as the Milburn and the Baker used mechanical relays and resistors placed between the batteries and motor to control speeds. This method varied the voltage going to the motor by using a combination of "parallel" or "series" battery connections to obtain desired voltages. The first speed might combine all batteries in parallel to produce 12 volts, other speeds would use all batteries in a different combination to produce 24 to 36 volts, and higher speeds would be obtained by placing the batteries in series to produce 48 volts or more, depending upon the number of 6-volt batteries the vehicle could carry.

The type of switch used to interconnect batteries is called a relay or solenoid. The solenoid is nothing more than a very heavy duty switch that can accept the high load requirements of electric vehicle power. Inside the solenoid is a coil of wire wrapped around an iron piston type device which, when electrically activated, causes the piston to close a switch electromagnetically. Combinations of solenoid relays can yield a variety of voltages for electric vehicle's speed requirements.

Unfortunately, the surge of power from the lowest voltage selection causes undesirable starting because of the tendency to jerk from a standstill. To lessen this problem, a resistance is provided by placing resistors in the circuit for the first speed. The use of resistors is an inefficient expedient. The resistor heats up because it is diverting some of the energy that would normally propel the vehicle.

A contemporary electric automobile, the Sebring-Vanguard CitiCar, uses a three-speed voltage regulation method. The first speed is achieved by parallel combinations to obtain 36 volts from the battery pack, which consists of eight 6-volt batteries. A nichrome resistor reduces the actual voltage to 18 volts. The second speed is achieved using 36 volts parallel again, this time without using the nichrome resistor. The third speed is achieved by a combination of series connections to obtain 48 volts for the maximum top speed of 38 mph (61 km/hr).

A newly designed CitiCar II will use a solid state infinitely-variable speed control, with the addition of a special switch for high speed bursts. Many electric vehicles use solid state systems, the most common of which is the SCR (silicon controlled rectifier.) Another type of solid state control is the "thyristor" which is similar to the SCR, in that it is an electronic device using semi-conductor material. The SCR, the most popular semi-conductor controller, is commonly referred to as a "chopper" because it quite literally chops the battery current into pieces to be fed to the motor as speed requirements dictate.

Up to 1,000 power pulses per second switch the motor on and off repeatedly. Depending upon the controller, the pulse "on" time and the frequency of "on" times are varied. These power pulses to the motor can theoretically produce smooth acceleration up to top speeds. Unfortunately, some tests indicate that in actual use, at very low speeds, the chopper produces a shuddering effect as the battery current is pulsed in nominal amounts to the motor. Work

is being conducted to design ever-improving control systems using solid state technology.

Early electric choppers have been SCR units exclusively, because transistors have not been capable of handling the larger currents required for vehicle use. New transistorized systems are being developed that will be able to meet vehicle needs. One advantage of transistors over SCR or thyristors is that while the SCR can pulse up to 1,000 times per second, the transistor can pulse up to 20,000 times per second. This could alleviate the shuddering at lower speeds.

For electric vehicles which have short range, low speed, and moderate power requirements, the simple parallel-series, stepped controllers are the best solution. Lightweight vehicles such as golf carts find the cheaper stepped controls perfectly adequate. But heavier and faster vehicles need the flexibility of the 97%-efficient solid state devices. The separately excitable field and armature of the compound wound or shunt wound DC motor currently offer benefits of high flexibility in conjunction with SCR chopper control.

In some cases, the power regulation method of speed control is not suitable for optimum performance. In these cases, the addition of a multiple-speed mechanical transmission may be needed. This depends upon the design of the vehicle and its intended use. Generally speaking, a multi-speed transmission is desirable in an electric vehicle because it can reduce the high current drain needed for difficult terrain. While it is true that a transmission is unnecessary for moderate-use vehicles, the needs of a versatile electric car are more demanding.

The high cost of SCR controls have rendered them impractical for some forms of electric transportation. Such is the case in electric bicycle conversion kits, which use a single forward speed on-and-off switch for control. The cost of SCR controls will become more economical as more are manufactured.

Another area of controls which deserves attention is braking. All electric vehicles are equipped with mechanical brakes, whether they be disc or drum, mechanical or hydraulic. But there is another type of braking which can extend battery life by using the force generated by the stopping vehicle to partially recharge the battery system. This type of braking is called "regenerative". The SCR chopper control can be used to strengthen the field current of a shunt- wound motor during deceleration. The motor is now converted into a generator and current is delivered to the battery.

Regenerative braking is designed to provide an extended range of the vehicle. Theoretically, 10 to 40% energy retrieval is possible. Driving cycles with frequent acceleration and deceleration benefit the most from regenerative braking. Another benefit of regenerative braking is that it improves penetration of the electrolyte into the grid material of a lead-acid battery. Effectively, battery life and efficiency are increased.

A regenerative braking system used on the Mars II made by the Electric Fuel Propulsion Company of Detroit uses an alternator attached to the drive motor. This regenerative system alone can stop the vehicle in about 500 feet (152 m) from a speed of 30 mph (48 km/hr).

One forklift manufacturer noted that substantial driver training was necessary to achieve desired regenerative braking yields. Vehicles designed with regenerative braking often have a dual brake system where the first position of the brake pedal yields regeneration and subsequent pressure provides both regeneration to its maximum and the application of mechanical brakes. Also a deceleration sensation can be incorporated into the design by engaging regeneration when the driver's foot is removed from the accelerator pedal.

Another form of braking which is occasionally used is "dynamic" braking. This basically has the effect of regenerative braking, except that the voltage produced by the motor acting as a generator does not have to be greater than the battery voltage. So braking action can be extended to a lower speed than with normal regenerative braking. The energy produced by dynamic braking is dissipated through a resistor bank which requires very large resistors. Because this system does not offer the recovery of kinetic energy and because it adds to the vehicle's complexity, it is generally not recommended as an auxiliary braking system.

Whether the mechanical brakes which must be incorporated into any vehicle design are drum or disc, either shoe or disc pad retractors must be used to prevent drag and useless energy waste.

In some control systems "free wheeling" or coasting is used to extend range. In this case the motor is disconnected. Free wheeling ceases when the brake is applied. The regenerative braking circuit is then energized followed by the engagement of the mechanical brakes.

Vehicles of the Present

There are few forms of transportation that can compare with the quietness, grace, and elegance of an electrical vehicle; a phenomenon matched only by sailboating, skydiving, and skiing.

Electric vehicles in use today are not as rare as one might expect. Many mass transportation systems use electric trains, which are efficient and pollution-free. The passenger of any office building elevator is actually riding in an electric vehicle, and most people are unaware that cross-country diesel trains are actually electric powered. Their diesel engines are used to run generators that produce electricity and supply power to electric motors which drive their wheels. The average person unknowingly comes into contact with electric vehicles every day.

The manner in which electric vehicles affect the lives of the people of the world is evidenced by their diverse functions. While electric automobiles remain an oddity in the contemporary transportation structure, certain fields are definitely the domain of electric power. Two examples are the electric forklift (which outnumbers its internal combustion counterparts), and electric golf carts.

chapter 6

In many urban situations, electric automobiles of even the most modest levels of development can meet today's acceleration and cruising speed requirements. Because much of urban traffic operates in the 10 to 20-mph (16 to 32 km/hr) range, a 60 or 70-mph (97 or 113 km/hr) top speed seems unnecessary. An electric vehicle with a 30-mph (48 km/hr) top speed can accelerate with conventional vehicles without becoming an obstruction to traffic or safety. The controls of an electric vehicle are similar to those of a modern automobile. There is no problem adapting the operator to new driving habits. However, the owner of an electric vehicle will have to adopt a style that is conservation-oriented, because electricity cannot be stored in abundance. Practice and familiarity with this problem will allow the driver to adapt with no more discomfort than the difference between moving from a luxury sedan to an economy model.

The modern vehicle designer is faced with problems that were unheard of a decade ago. He is conscious of dwindling energy reserves and aware of restrictive federal requirements for safety, emissions, and performance. Today's electric vehicle technology is adequate to meet many of these requirements.

When I first began researching this subject, I noticed that electric vehicles had been abandoned by a number of companies during the 1920's era. It seemed odd that one company after another had fallen victim to the proliferation of the gasoline vehicle. A company had to divert its efforts to internal combustion models or face bankruptcy. Unfortunately, I observed a similar recurrence when I tried to contact electric vehicle companies which had operated businesses within the past five years. A significant number of my letters were returned with the notation "Address Unknown" or "Moved." It seems the entrepreneural nature of electric vehicle production is a rocky road. These business ventures included efforts that range from sports cars, vans, and electric motor scooters to commercial vehicles.

Even well-publicized production vehicles, such as the Sebring Vanguard CitiCar, and the Elcar, an Italian import produced by Zagato, have not received high public acclaim. Although it remains true that any electric car will still draw a sizeable crowd of "gawkers," the fact remains that the average person, spoiled by the large luxury passenger automobile replete with air conditioning, power steering and brakes, electric seats and other accoutrements, will not accept a small commuter electric vehicle as an interim solution to gas shortages, even as a second car.

In truth, the small, four-cylinder import that achieves 35 to 40 miles (56 to 64 km) per gallon on the highway still provides economy, handling, and creature comforts which are difficult for an electric automobile manufacturer to match. There are no electric automobile prototypes that can equal the acceleration, economy, cruising speed and general wherewithal of a Volkswagen Rabbit. Development of the Rabbit is a result of many millions of dollars invested in research and production.

The plight of a new electric commuter vehicle is, therefore, to be compared against tried and true, successful, and publicly-accepted vehicles that have endured more than twenty years of automotive history.

Any interim design that is to be embraced by the public will need a strong impetus to warrant participation. Perhaps gasoline prices in the

United States of two dollars per gallon may trigger a public awareness of economy and conservation and thus may contribute to electric vehicle acceptance.

One manufacturer has oriented his designs toward the luxury vehicle market shared by Mercedes and Rolls Royce. The "Transformer One" electric, luxury, sports sedan which sells for over $30,000 brings to mind the golden days of the expensive electric carriages designed to service the very wealthy. But the optimum electric vehicle must be an economy-oriented, four-passenger commuter sedan, priced in the $4,000 to $5,000 range, to be competitive in those markets secured by Toyota, Datsun, Honda, and Volkswagen.

Our "Vehicles of Today" chapter does not include every vehicle produced in the world currently. Every year new prototypes and designs for production vehicles emanate from the United States, England, Japan, France, Germany, and other countries interested in this growing field. By the time this book goes to press, there may be production vehicles offered to the public that will differ greatly from those listed. However, the reader will be in a position to appreciate the coming of a new generation of vehicles.

One thing is certain—even as I write this, somebody out there will be putting the finishing touches on a prototype in hopes of attracting financial backing to enter the market. The texture of this new field will be determined by those companies that fulfill the public's need. No one can predict which company will be chosen by the public as its standard bearer. Solutions may come from the small dynamic producer geared expressly for electric vehicle design, or it may be an offshoot of the "Big 3" automakers in the United States. Or possibly a Japanese manufacturer, who will unveil a completely-tested entry, boxed and packaged for immediate consumption.

PLEASE NOTE: Vehicle specifications have been obtained from the manufacturer or from other published sources. Because we have not formally tested each vehicle shown, we must rely upon the manufacturers' good intentions regarding published specifications.

Inquiries regarding specific vehicles should be directed to the manufacturer.

ELECTRIC AUTOMOTIVE DEVELOPMENT IN AMERICA
Sebring-Vanguard

There are about 2,000 electric automobiles produced and sold to date in the United States. One of the most popular of these vehicles is the Sebring-Vanguard CitiCar, the first mass-produced electric automobile in America. The Sebring Vanguard Company is based in Columbia, Md., and has been producing electrics for over three years. This vehicle received much publicity after its introduction in 1974 and for a time was selling as many as could be produced.

The CitiCar looks a little bit like a cross between a golf cart and a telephone booth and is a courageous effort to enter into an infant market with a fully functioning product.

Energy storage for the CitiCar is accomplished by eight 6-volt traction deep cycle batteries. Power is transmitted through a series-wound DC General Electric motor, producing 3.5 horsepower. One test report of the 1,250 pound (567 kg) CitiCar yielded a zero to 30 mph (48 km/hr) time of 13.9 seconds and a top speed of 38 mph (61 km/hr).

The CitiCar I uses a combination of voltages to the motor to achieve various speeds. The first speed uses 24 volts parallel (all batteries) with a nichrome resistor. The second speed uses 24 volts parallel without the nichrome resistor, and the third speed uses 48 volts series. The forward-reverse control is on the dashboard and is operated by a toggle switch with a safety neutral position. The city driving cycle is rated at an electricity consumption of 3.5 miles (5.6 km) per kilowatt hour. Maximum range of the CitiCar is 40 to 50 miles (64 to 80 km). The maximum range per day with intermittent charging is rated at 100 miles (161 km).

The CitiCar is also available as a CitiVan which is a lightweight utility truck conversion. The CitiVan uses a 6-hp 4,100-rpm air-cooled, series-wound DC motor. The power source is eight 6-volt deep-cycle batteries with a total rated voltage of 48 volts. The projected battery cycle life is 400 to 600 full recharges. The body is a rust and corrosion proof impact resistant plastic; the frame is aluminum. Total curb weight is 1,360 lbs. (618 kg) with a suggested list price of about $4,000.

The CitiVan and CitiCar are both ideal for duty such as mail delivery. One CitiVan was sold to the U.S. Postal Service R. & D. Center at Rockville, Md.

Photo courtesy of Sebring Vanguard

The Long Island Lighting Company of New York began an electric vehicle demonstration program on April 4, 1977, to test and evaluate the practicality, performance and efficiency of the electric vehicle for meter reading and as "second car" transportation. In addition, this program was designed to encourage other vehicle fleet owners to use electric automobiles for duties such as meter reading, patrols by police, security, and delivery. Long Island Lighting Company purchased two CitiCars initially and their success has prompted an order for eighteen additional vehicles.

Another experiment is the Salt River Project (SRP) which is the power utility for Phoenix, Arizona. The three CitiCars were used in a demonstration during July, August and September of 1976, during which time 7,300 total miles (11,748 km) were driven by SRP employees in a variety of service duties.

Mr. Robert Beaumont of Sebring-Vanguard acknowledges that, although improvements have been made since the CitiCar's introduction in 1974, there is still room for more development. He also pointed out that eighteen years elapsed between the development of Ford's Model T and Model A (although one must remember that over fifteen million Model T's were produced versus the CitiCar's 2,000).

One CitiCar customer from Washington, D.C., surpassed the 17,000 mile (27,358 km) mark on his 1974 CitiCar, with many more owners in the over-10,000 mile (16,093 km) category. As with any limited-edition vehicle, the CitiCar is subject to auto cultists who treat fellow owners like long lost relatives. Effectively every owner is a pioneer in this newly-rediscovered phenomenon.

A redesigned CitiCar II will meet all federal motor safety standards and will be a significantly improved design. A new solid-state control system will provide variable speeds, smoother and faster acceleration, higher efficiency and will include a device which will allow a top speed of 44 mph (71 km/hr). The claimed effective range of the new vehicle will be 50 to 60 miles (80 to 96 km) with a normal cruising speed of 38 mph (61 km/hr).

Photo courtesy of
General Engines, Inc.

The Comuta-Car and Comuta-Van

In 1978 the General Engines Co., of Sewell, New Jersey, acquired the assets of Sebring-Vanguard and is now producing two vehicles called the Comuta-Car and the Comuta-Van.

While both vehicles ostensibly resemble the original Sebring-Vanguard models, and retain the exact top speed and cruising range, significant improvements have been made.

The front and rear bumpers have been constructed of a shock absorbing material and mechanical shock absorbers have been fitted to render them "legal" under U.S. safety regulations. The braking system has been redesigned. The suspension system has been re-engineered and the frame has been reinforced by being fully "gussetted."

General Engines has established a network of dealers to sell and maintain their products. For more information about their entire line of electric cars, trucks, bikes and trikes, contact: General Engines, Inc. Commuter Vehicles Division, 591 Mantua Blvd., Sewell, New Jersey, U.S.A. 08080

Photo Courtesy of General Engines, Inc.

The Electro-Sport

The General Engines Co. also offers a full scale electric replica of a 1929 Mercedes-Benz roadster called the Electro-Sport. This custom sports runabout is built to order as a limited production model.

The Electro-Sport uses a 4-speed manual shift, 72 V. series wound D.C. motor and carries twelve 6 V. "deep cycle" golf cart batteries weighing 62 lbs (28 kg) each. Top speed is 50 mph (80 km/hr) with a 45 mph (72 km/hr) cruising speed. Range is 50 miles (80 km) per charge. Vehicle weight is 1690 lbs (768 kg).

For more information contact: General Engines, Inc., Commuter Vehicles Division, 591 Mantua Blvd., Sewell, New Jersey, U.S.A. 08080

Photos courtesy of Electric Fuel Propulsion, Inc.

Transformer I

The Transformer I is a $30,000 luxury electric-powered automobile produced by Electric Fuel Propulsion Corporation (EFP), Detroit, Michigan. Features such as leather interior, air conditioning, stereo tape deck, powered seats, power brakes and electric windows are among the accessories available. The Transformer I has a top speed of 70 mph (113 km/hr) and cruising speed of 55 mph (88 km/hr). Acceleration is zero to 30 mph (48 km/hr) in 8 seconds. Power is stored in a 180-volt tri-polar lead-cobalt battery system. A 32 volt DC motor is used with a solid-state electronic controller.

The lead-cobalt battery system is patented by Mr. Robert R. Aronson, inventor, founder and president of Electric Fuel Propulsion Corporation. It is claimed that the lead-cobalt battery has more than twice the energy per pound than ordinary lead-acid batteries and can store new energy six times faster. The lead-cobalt battery can be charged to 80% capacity in approximately 45 minutes using a "fast- charge" system. Normal lead-acid batteries could not survive constant fast recharging at this rate, but the cobaltous sulphate with other chemicals enables quick charging of 400 to 500 amps DC without harmful oxidation or production of toxic gases. EFP rates their battery at a 50,000-mile (80,467-km) life and an 18-watt- hours/lb (40-wh/kg) rating, which is attractive by today's standards. Battery replacement is estimated at $1,500 at today's prices, and the electric motor has a projected life of over 20 years.

For long trips, a trailer-mounted gasoline-powered generator is an optional piece of equipment. The five-passenger car uses a standard General Motors two-door mid-sized body. Future model considerations include a Transformer II four-door sedan, based on the Cadillac Seville.

Mobile Power Plant

A mobile generator makes it possible to cover hundreds of miles of expressway driving an eight-hour day with a quick booster charge at lunch time. By hitching the EFP mobile power plant, the Transformer I can yield up to 1,100 miles (1,770 km) a day (equalling 22 hours of driving at 50 mph (80 km/hr) with two hours for refueling. Normal driving range is stated as 100 miles with an occasional midday supplemental charge.

EFP History

In 1970, the EFP Electric Hornet won the Electric Class of the Clean Air Car Race which was a seven day event. Also, the components of the Electric Fuel Propulsion Corporation were used in the CalTech Vehicle from the Great Electric Car Race as noted in the History Chapter.

The electrified Hornet used a 20-hp electric motor, 24 batteries and had a top speed of 79.2 mph (128 km/hr). The vehicle weighed 5,500 lbs. (2495 kg) and utilized a solid state controller.

An earlier Electric Fuel Propulsion Vehicle was called the Mars II and was a converted Renault R-10 weighing 3,640 lb (1651 kg) which carried 1,700 lbs (771 kg) of batteries. The car featured a regenerative braking system and utilized a 15-hp direct-current motor which could accelerate from zero to 40 mph (64 km) in 10 seconds and reach a top speed of 60 mph (97 km/hr) with a 70 to 120 mile (113 to 193 km) range from lead-cobalt batteries. Recharge cycles claimed for the lead-cobalt batteries were

800, which would be the equivalent of driving up to 90,000 miles (144,840 km) per battery set. Normal cruising speed was 45 to 55 mph (72 to 89 km/hr). In a test, on October 6, 1967, the Mars II traveled 2,000 miles (3219 kg) across the U.S.

EFP MARS II   Photo courtesy of Electric Fuel Propulsion, Inc.

EFP ELECTRIC HORNET   Photo courtesy of Electric Fuel Propulsion, Inc.

METRO

Photos courtesy of Electric Vehicles Associates, Inc.

"CHANGE OF PACE" WAGON

"CHANGE OF PACE" SEDAN

E.V.A.

Electric Vehicle Associates, Inc., Cleveland, Ohio (EVA), manufactures electric vehicles for fleet and individual use. A previous model, the Metro, was based on the Renault 12 TL body, and powered by nineteen 6-volt batteries. The vehicle had a cruising speed of 55 mph (89 km/hr), with a range of 30 to 55 miles (48 to 89 km) per charge. This compact, 4-door sedan had automatic transmission, power steering, and power disc brakes. The control system was a SCR solid-state control with battery and motor protection. Vehicle weight is 3,150 lbs. (1,429 kg), including battery charger. Projected cost of operation totals 3.5¢ per mile of which 1.3¢ is for electricity and 2.1¢ battery replacement cost. Also included is 0.1¢ for distilled water which is consumed at a rate of 500 miles per gallon (805 km).

The current vehicle is the "Change of Pace" electric station wagon. This basic American Motors production Pacer model is converted to electric power and has a top speed in excess of 55 mph (89 km/hr) and a range of 40 to 60 miles (64 to 97 km/hr) per charge. Zero to 30 miles (0 to 48 km) per hour performance is 12 seconds. The curb weight of the vehicle is about 4,150 lbs. (1,882 kg) carrying an on-board 110 or 240-volt battery charger.

For more information write EVA, 9100 Bank St., Cleveland, Ohio 44125.

Photo courtesy of the Electric Auto Corporation

E.A.C. Silver Volt

The Silver Volt is a 4-passenger station wagon which features a continuously variable transmission, transistorized controller, power steering, power brakes, and air conditioning.

The patented lead-cobalt tri-polar battery pack weighs 1800 lbs (818 kg) and yields a range of 63 miles (101 km) in an SAE J227A Metropolitan driving cycle. At a constant 30 mph (48 km/hr), range is 105 miles (168 km) per charge. Maximum speed is 70 mph (113 km/hr) and cruising speed is 55 mph (89 km/hr).

The Silver Volt carries an on-board EFP gasoline generator which powers the air conditioning, power steering, power brakes, and provides extension of operating range as a series-hybrid.

The Electric Auto Corporation plans to market the Silver Volt as a production model in 1980. For more information, contact The Electric Auto Corporation, 2237 Elliott Ave., Troy, Michigan 48084, U.S.A.

Photo courtesy of Braunlich-Roessle

Braun Elec

The Braun Elec is a design based on the Honda 600 body. It is built by Braunlich-Roessle, Pittsburgh, Pa. A top speed of 45 mph (72 km/hr) and range of 35 miles (56 km) are obtained from a 36-volt battery system and 10.3 hp electric motor. This front-wheel-drive vehicle attains economy of 1¢ per mile operating cost. It was built as a prototype to explore the feasibility of manufacturing a production model.

Photo courtesy of
Copper Development Association

Copper Development Association

Copper Electric Town Car—A dramatic and streamlined electric vehicle of advanced prototype design conceived by the Copper Development Association, Inc., the copper and brass industry's advanced market development arm.

The electric Town Car has a range of 103 miles (165.8 km) at a cruising speed of 40 mph (64 km/hr) and a 73.3 mile (118 km) range in start-and-stop city driving. Acceleration is a brisk zero to 30 mph (48 km/hr) in 8.8 seconds, with a top speed of 59 miles per hour (95 km/hr). The two- seater hatchback model uses existing components and innovative technology, and is designed for optimum range. The 2,952 lb (1339 kg) vehicle carries approximately 1,200 lbs (544 km) of batteries with battery weight expected to be reduced when state-of-the-art batteries become more efficient. To minimize mechanical friction, radial tires and other measures were used. To assure low wind resistance, a streamlined shape, smooth underpan, flush windows and windshield wipers concealed by a flush panel were incorporated into the design.

The eighteen 6-volt lead-acid storage batteries can be recharged overnight. The motor is specially wound, separately excited, and matched to a control system which provides the highest possible efficiency using production components.

The Copper Development Association, Inc., produced this vehicle to keynote the unique properties of copper in electric vehicle production. Copper and copper alloys are used in motor windings, battery cables, and a variety of components which are a valuable contribution to the production considerations of electric vehicles.

Copper alloy tubing used for hydraulic brake lines and copper alloy brake drums are used in all four wheels. This vehicle also incorporates regenerative braking. In a suburban cycle of two stops per mile, reaching 35 mph (56 km/hr), the range without regenerative braking was 68.7 miles (110.6 km) per charge, compared to 73.3 miles (118.0 km) per charge with regenerative braking.

Photo courtesy of Copper Development Association

Copper Electric Runabout

To date, the Copper Development Association has conceived six electric vehicle projects, the latest of which, the Copper Electric Runabout, is a new four passenger automobile with several distinct advantages over the Copper Electric Town Car (see preceding page).

The Runabout's most noteworthy feature is the four passenger, three door design configuration, with the rear-seat occupants facing rearwards. This vehicle can be described as "short but roomy," and built tall to eliminate the psychological feeling of smallness.

The body is constructed of fiberglass reinforced polyester. The chassis includes a "backbone" design which houses the batteries in the center of the vehicle. The 12 advanced lead-acid batteries are manufactured by Globe-Union and weigh 822 lbs (373 kg). Total vehicle weight is 2,152 lbs (980 kg), which is about one third lighter than the Copper Electric Town Car.

The 14 hp (1 hour rating) motor can accelerate the vehicle from 0-30 mph (48 km/hr) in 8.6 seconds. Top speed is 59 mph (95 km/hr), and the cruising range is 72 miles (116 km) at a constant 40 mph (64 km/hr). A city driving cycle of two stops per mile with a 35 mph (56 km/hr) maximum speed between stops yielded a 79 mile (127 km) range.

Globe-Union Maxima

The Globe-Union Maxima is a prototype five passenger station wagon designed as a test bed for Globe batteries.

Top speed is up to 75 mph (120 km/hr) using a 20 hp General Electric Motor and 240 volt electrical system consisting of twenty specially formulated deep cycle 12 volt batteries. Total vehicle weight is 4,350 lbs (1978 kg).

Globe-Union, Inc. is the world's largest manufacturer of "replacement" automotive batteries.

Photo courtesy of Globe-Union, Inc.

Photo courtesy of the General Electric Company

The G.E. Centennial Electric

The Centennial Electric was built to honor the 100th birthday of the General Electric Company. This sleek, low-slung, experimental four passenger sedan will serve as a test bed for General Electric products. Although the company does not plan to market the vehicle, it is prepared to supply automobile manufacturers with G.E. motors, solid state controllers, and other essential components.

The front-wheel drive subcompact was designed "from the ground up" using commercially available off-the-shelf components and battery systems.

A 24 hp G.E. motor and 18 Globe-Union advanced lead acid batteries, mounted in a centrally located chassis tunnel, supply the power through a G.E. Solid-State controller. The vehicle features a stainless steel underbody and chassis and a hatchback for rear seat passengers. Total weight, including batteries, is 3,250 lbs (1500 kg).

The stop-and-go range is 45 miles (72 km) based on the SAE-J227a/D driving cycle. At a constant 40 mph (64 km/hr), the vehicle can travel 75 miles on a single charge. Accelleration is 0-30 mph (48 km/hr) in nine seconds, and top speed is 60 mph (97 km/hr).

The Centennial Electric was built to G.E.

specifications by Triad Services of Dearborn, Michigan, USA. Triad Services is an engineering design company headed by Michael A. Pocobello, who is responsible for many electric vehicle prototypes including the Copper Development Van and the Copper Electric Town Car.

Photo courtesy of the General Electric Company

Eighteen Globe-Union advanced lead-acid batteries, weighing 1,225 lbs (555 kg), are stored in a movable trolley in the centrally located chassis tunnel.

Sears, Roebuck and Co., U.S.A.—"XDH-1"

In the early days of automobile pioneering, the Sears Roebuck Company produced a variety of motor carriages which competed for the market of gasoline-powered cars. Eventually, the company divested itself of their automobile production division because they found there was more money to be made selling parts for Henry Ford's "Model T."

In 1953, Sears introduced the "Allstate." This automobile was a version of the Kaiser "Henry J" compact model, and was the last attempt for a Sears bid into the automobile production industry.

Today, Sears has put its name on an experimental electric automobile—not for the purpose of introducing a new model, but as a means to promote its line of "DieHard" batteries.

The "XDH-1," which means "experimental DieHard number one," is a reconstructed Italian Fiat 128-3P weighing 3,110 lbs (1411 kg).

Sears claims no intention of marketing an electric automobile in the forseeable future, and has no ties with the Fiat company.

The XDH-1 is powered by twenty Sears Die-Hard experimental electric vehicle batteries.

This front-wheel-drive vehicle carries five batteries in front and fifteen in the rear. Cruising range is 90 miles (145 km) at 47 mph (76 km/hr). A four-speed transmission with clutch allows speeds of up to 75 mph (121 km/hr) using a compound-wound 120-volt World War II airplane starter motor rated at 40 hp peak. Other features include a solid state controller and regenerative braking.

Photo courtesy of Sears Roebuck and Company

Photos courtesy of Dr. H.D. Kesling

Kesling Yare

The Yare is a totally streamlined, $60,000 proto-type vehicle built by Dr. H.D. Kesling, of Westville, Indiana, U.S.A.

It has an elongated, egg-shaped appearance and its four wheels are arranged in a diamond pattern. The front and back wheels, centrally located, are used for steering; power is applied to

the side wheels, which are just slightly rear of center. As the vehicle steers, the body tilts in one direction, which results in one side being six to ten inches higher than the other. This feature also allows easy entrance to the vehicle.

The "Yare" is a nautical term, meaning complete, eager, lively, prepared, fit to move, easily worked, manageable and active.

Performance yields a 55 mph speed (88 km/hr) in 12 seconds from a 12 hp motor. The 72-volt battery pack produces a range of over 50 miles (80 km) per charge. The total weight is 2,300 lbs (1043 kg), with a height of only 52 inches (130 cm).

Dr. Kesling believes that if this car were put into production it would sell for about $4,000, and that it would conceivably be produced by a boat manufacturer rather than an auto maker.

The twelve 6-volt golf cart batteries are positioned in the frame as shown. The power plant of the vehicle is a tricycle formed by the two side wheels and the rear wheel, which can be disconnected in a few minutes from the body. Seating arrangement makes it possible for three adults and two children to ride comfortably in the "hull."

Photo courtesy of Electric Passenger Cars, Inc.

E.P.C. Hummingbird

Electric Passenger Cars, Inc., San Diego, California, has developed three Hummingbird models.

The original "Hummingbird I" was a prototype based on the Volkswagen 181 "Thing" body style.

A second development prototype, the "Hummingbird II," is based on the Volkswagen Rabbit body style. This model weighs 2,570 lbs (1165 kg) and uses twelve 6-volt lead-acid batteries and a 15-hp series-wound motor to yield a range of 50 miles (80 km) at 40 mph (64 km/hr) with a top speed of 52 mph (84 km/hr).

A new production prototype, the "Hummingbird Hybrid MkI," is now undergoing testing. This model uses advanced batteries and an on-board gasoline generator to extend range. Minimum hybrid performance capabilities are: top speed—65 mph (105 km/hr), zero to 30 mph (48 km/hr) in 10 seconds. Range is up to 150 miles (241 km) at 35 mph (56 km/hr). Stop-and-start city cycle is 100 miles (161 km). A new Electromatic transmission is being developed which will allow regenerative braking and even greater energy savings.

Another new EPC model is the "Hummingbird Hybrid KSV," which will use a patented "crash-proof" safety body.

For more information write: Electric Passenger Cars, Inc., 5127 Galt Way, San Diego, California 92117, U.S.A.

Photo courtesy of Die Mesh Corp.

Die Mesh Spider

The experimental Die Mesh Spider is based on a 1972 converted FIAT 850. Three 3.2 hp electric motors produce a top speed of 55 mph (88 km/hr). The power pack of 18 lead-acid batteries provides a 42 mile (67 km) range. Total vehicle weight is 2850 lbs (1292 kg).

Die Mesh has been involved with electric vehicle research since 1968. One development is an infinitely variable traction transmission which permits continually variable output speeds from a constant input speed.

B & Z Electric Car

The B & Z Electric Car Company of Signal Hill, California, U.S.A., produces the B & Z electric car, which is a three- or four-wheel, two-passenger, two-door coupe. They also produce a "Rancho," 1/4-ton pickup truck, a "Long Rancho" 1/2-ton pickup and the four passenger "Surrey." Each vehicle is custom made to suit individual requirements.

The B & Z car has a top speed of 18 to 32 mph (29 to 52 km/hr) depending on the horsepower of the motor selected. Motors range from 1 to 3-1/2 horsepower. The standard battery pack is 336 lbs (152 kg) with additional battery packs available. The range is 22 to 56 miles per charge (35 to 90 km), depending on battery selection.

720-B Town Coupe

The 720-B Town Coupe is produced by Bee Engineering Company of Westminster, California. This production electric sedan features an 8 HP, 72 volt traction motor with a torque sensitive automatic transmission and transistorized control. Top speed is 40 MPH (64 km/hr), range is 40 to 60 miles (64 to 97 km). This vehicle was designed from the ground up, employing state-of-the-art technology. For more information write Bee Engineering, 9643 Bolsa Avenue, Westminster, California 92683.

The Free-Way Electric

High Mileage Vehicles of Apple Valley, Minnesota, produces a variety of three wheel vehicles called Free Way models. The Free Way is manufactured in both gasoline and electric versions and in two body types: The "Deluxe" and the open bodied "Economy" model.

Both Free-Way Electrics share the same running gear and fiberglass body. Top speed is 56 mph (90 km/hr) maximum. At a 40 mph (64 km/hr) crusing speed the range is 50 miles (80 km). Total vehicle weight is 625 lbs (284 kg).

For more information about all Free-Way models and how to obtain their book entitled "High Mileage Vehicles a New Technology," write: H-M Vehicles, Inc., 6276 Greenleaf Trail, Apple Valley, Mn. 55124 U.S.A.

ECONOMY "FREE-WAY"

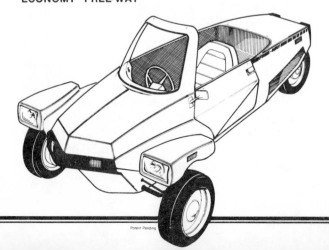

DELUXE "FREE-WAY"

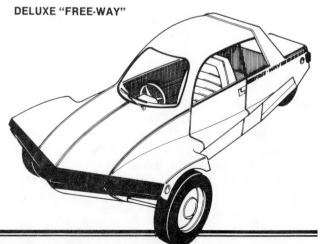

Photo courtesy of C.H. Waterman Industries

Electricar 1

The Electricar 1 is a four passenger electric car produced by C. H. Waterman Industries. This compact two-door sedan is an electric conversion of the Renault LeCar series. Top speed is 55 mph (88 km/hr), cruising speed is 45 mph (72 km/hr) and acceleration is 0-30 mph (48 km/hr) in 15 seconds. Range is 60-80 miles (96-128 km) using sixteen 6 volt electric vehicle batteries. The Electricar 1 uses a 48 volt DC traction motor and two step foot operated speed control.

This vehicle is available to the public as a production automobile. For more information write C. H. Waterman Industries, 502 Park Avenue, New York, New York 10022.

Photos courtesy of General Motors Corp.

Chevrolet Electrovette

The Electrovette is the first of a new series of electric test cars produced by the General Motors Corp. This experimental prototype uses twenty 12-volt maintenance-free batteries weighing 920 lbs. (417 kg) which are carried in the rear seat compartment. The suspension system has been re-engineered to handle the additional weight. The two passenger sedan weighs 2,950 lbs (1338 kg) and has a top speed of 53 mph (85 km/hr). Acceleration is zero to 30 mph (48 km/hr) in 8.2 seconds. The range using lead-acid batteries is 50 miles (80 km) at 30 mph (48 km/hr). (This is about the same distance as a normal Chevette can travel on one gallon of gasoline.) In September, 1979, General Motors announced that their zinc-nickel oxide batteries will double the range in the near future. G.M. lithium/iron sulfide batteries which are smaller, lighter and more powerful may be 10-15 years down the road unless technological breakthroughs can shorten the time span. The Electrovette uses an on-board computer which is a control signal processor and the "brain" of the system.

U.S. ELECTRIC TRUCKS

Today, there is a large potential market for electric pickup and delivery trucks. Commercial vehicles can begin to reduce the consumption of gasoline and lower urban pollution in the immediate future.

The economics are better for fleet ownership than individual ownership in the electric truck industry. Fleet-size operations using ten or more vehicles and delivery circuits with stop-and-start driving of forty to fifty miles (64 to 80 km) per day are best suited for this application. The upkeep necessary for these vehicles would be accomplished by the same facility now used for an existing fleet. Maintenance would largely serve battery needs, while the mechanical maintenance should be low as indicated by the dependability record of electric vehicles in general.

Some applications most suited include wholesale/retail deliveries, food processors, parcel and mail delivery, rental trucks, gas and electric utility service, and small business applications such as bakeries, florists, and pizza delivery.

"GoLIAth"—A Giant Step Forward for Electric Vehicle Development."

In the U.S., one of the leaders in the promotion and dissemination of electric vehicle information to the industry and public has been the LIA (Lead Industries Association). The LIA has mounted a continuing effort to build a market

Photo courtesy of Lead Industries Association

and, more importantly, an acceptance of electric cars, buses, and trucks by the general public.

The LIA designed a program to provide needed electric vehicle information by facing some of the problems of on-the-road electric delivery vehicles.

To implement this program, LIA joined forces with the electric utility industry and one of its own trade groups, The Electric Vehicle Council (EVC). The LIA brainchild manifested itself in the form of a lightweight, battery-operated truck appropriately named the "GoLIAth."

The LIA GoLIAth was designed as a test bed around lead-acid batteries to exhibit the appropriateness of this type of energy system for short-haul multiple stop, pick-up, and delivery chores. Data was also designed to include personal transportation routes and commercial- industrial applications.

January, 1974, marked the beginning of the year-long tour for GoLIAth. Starting in New York City and including 25 major cities in the United States and Canada, the GoLIAth proceeded to fulfill the three major objectives of the LIA program:

1. To determine the role that lead-acid batteries will play in the developing electric vehicle industry.
2. To determine the parameters of work-service situations which lend themselves to electric vehicle use.
3. To help determine the effect of electric vehicle delivery use on the load of electric utilities.

During the 2500-mile (4000 km) tour, GoLIAth's duties varied from tour exhibitions to operation in a variety of terrain and temperature conditions, with temperatures ranging from 10° to 105°F. (− 12 to 41 C).

GoLIAth dependably traveled up to 65 miles (104 km) per day at speeds from 25 to 30 mph (40 to 48 km/hr). Tests also demonstrated 150 stops and starts, as well as competitiveness to internal combustion vehicles at expressway speeds of up to 60 mph (97 km/hr).

Commonwealth Edison of Chicago, Illinois, used GoLIAth in a two-month test that shuttled passengers a distance of about 1½ miles (2.4 km). Statistics generated from the experiment indicated that the energy cost for electric vehicles is about half that of the presently-used vans. GoLIAth uses about one kilowatt hour (kwh) of electrical energy for each mile (1.6 km) traveled in congested downtown traffic. This would be the equivalent of about 2.7¢ per mile (1.7¢ per km) for commercial rate customers with vehicle recharging during off-peak hours. Even when the 2.3¢ per mile (1.4¢ per km) periodic battery replacement charge is added to the energy cost, the total is still 5¢ per mile (3.1¢ per km). A significant saving can be shown when one realizes that a conventional van at 56¢ per gallon and six miles per gallon (2.5 km/l) will have an energy cost of 9.3¢ per mile (5.7¢ per km).

Recently, LIA redesigned and reconstructed GoLIAth to incorporate the latest electric truck technology. The new GoLIAth II is literally a test lab on wheels. Features incorporated include new radial tires designed especially for lightweight trucks, and an advanced, more simplified electronic motor controller. The exterior of GoLIAth was also redesigned, with special attention given to wind drag by rounding contours and using wrap-around panels. The GoLIAth II was placed in service on April 5, 1977, with the National Capitol Region (NCR), a unit of the U.S. Department of Interiors National Park Service which operates and maintains national park sites in the area of Washington, D.C. This assignment will be a long-term demonstration program.

More than a dozen electrics are used for maintenance and personnel tasks for NCR. The variety of electric vehicle duties range from waste disposal and collection to general maintenance. Several units are designed to handle freight, while others are personnel carriers.

Other NCR electric vehicles include a twenty-passenger Electrobus for shuttle purposes, two Sebring-Vanguard Citicars for city routes, and one Aurenthetic Electric motorcycle for messenger purposes.

NCR also uses a hybrid utility truck which carries a five-horsepower internal combustion engine and has a range of 200 miles (322 km). Eventually the gasoline engine will be upgraded by using an experimental Stirling-Cycle engine under development. A Stirling-Cycle engine is an external combustion engine of advanced design which has been researched by Ford and other companies. The NCR fleet is committed to electric power and has a successful service record. An NCR electric passenger car logged 18,000 miles (28,968 km) in 25-mile (40 km) per day cycles demonstrating a good application of the Sebring-Vanguard Citicar for commercial use.

Demonstrations such as these are important.

One incidental study produced evidence that an increase of up to 13% can be achieved in electric vehicle performance if the driver is properly trained. In addition, battery charging patterns indicated that once-a-day charging was more economical than many daily charges.

A new vehicle called "GoLIAth III" was placed in service on June 20, 1977 with the First Pennsylvania Bank of Philadelphia to carry inter-office mail and bank personnel. Later GoLIAth III traveled through Chicago to work as a demonstration vehicle for one of Chicago's leading banks.

The results of these tests have been rewarding for the electric vehicle industry as a whole because it shows a determination that will, hopefully, lead to an earlier assimilation of the electric vehicle into our society.

The United States Postal Service Electric Vehicle Program

In the future, one major user of electric vehicles will be the U.S. Postal Service. If the current electric vehicle demonstration program now in effect continues to prove electric vehicle superiority, as many as 30,000 conventional vehicles (trucks, vans, and passenger cars) will be converted to electric power.

If these plans become a reality, there will be a large ongoing market for electric vehicles, with up to 15,000 new vehicles required each year.

Studies for electric postal vehicles began in 1971, using an English Harbilt Electric Van. In a Cupertino, California, operation, Harbilt trucks were in continuous use for two years, exhibiting about 1,800 vehicle-days of service with a total of only 33 days down time, as of September 1, 1977. In this test the vehicles were on the street less than five hours a day with about eleven miles per day average. Nevertheless, this constituted an annual mileage of about 3,200 miles (5,149 km).

The Harbilt Vans in the Cupertino test operated on 1.3 kilowatt hours per mile (.8¢ kwh/km). At 2.8¢ per kilowatt hour, fuel costs equalled about 3½¢ per mile (2.1¢ per km) compared to almost 6¢ (3.7¢ per km) for a comparable gasoline-powered vehicle. As gasoline prices go up, the disparity in price becomes more pronounced.

Because of the success of the Cupertino program, the U.S. Postal Service has purchased 350 additional electric vehicles built by A. M. General Corporation, which is a subsidiary of American Motors. The converted "Jeep type" vehicles were delivered from May, 1975, to March, 1976.

Of the 350 Jeeps 300 are operating in southern California, which is one of the nation's most

Photo courtesy of AM General Corp.

AM GENERAL POSTAL VAN

Photo courtesy of AM General Corp.

severe smog areas. Other vehicles were placed in diverse climates for testing purposes.

To date, the vehicles are performing with few problems and data will soon provide the program with annual costs based on fuel and maintenance.

Not all U.S. Post Office routes are suited for electric vehicles. However, a review by the post office indicates that at least 30,000 routes could be serviced by this type of vehicle.

Reports indicate the possible acquisition of 750 additional electric vans in fiscal 1978 by the postal service. Specifications will be issued and bids taken as soon as the cost analysis is cleared by the board of governors.

Let up hope that the future plans of the post office will include more of these electric vehicles, because they are ideally suited to many of the problems of the postal service and also reduce smog and emissions. Their use by the postal service would be a well-placed step forward as a foothold for the budding electric vehicle industry.

AM General Corporation

AM General Corporation is a subsidiary of American Motors located in Wayne, Michigan. In 1974, the company received a $2 million contract from the U.S. Post Office to design and produce 350 Electric Postal Delivery vehicles called the Electruc with a 500 lb (227 kg) payload capacity and top speed of 33 mph (53 km/hr). An Electruc can make 300 stops in five hours within a 20 mile (32 km) range. Maximum range is 30 miles (48 km). Cruising speed is up to 40 miles per hour (64 km/hr).

Eleven Electrucs were sold to divisions of American Telephone & Telegraph (AT&T), five of which operate at the telephone division of New York Bell. Other Electrucs were tested in Indiana and Minnesota, and one Electruc is in a demonstration program at Bell Laboratories in Murray Hill, New Jersey.

AM General Corporation is the first major U.S. company to produce electric vehicles in significant numbers.

Photo courtesy of Copper Development Association

Copper Electric Van IIIB

The Copper Development Association (CDA) sponsored the construction of the CDA Electric Van for the sole purpose of accumulating "in-use" data of electric truck application.

The CDA Van has been leased to the Water Meter Department of the City of Birmingham, Michigan, since November 13, 1973. It has been in daily use on assignments which relate to servicing water meters. The daily mileage ranges from 10 to 60 miles (16 to 96 km), totaling about 7,000 miles (11,250 km) per year.

Features of the experimental van include front-wheel drive, a 22-hp GE DC series motor, automatic transmission, fiberglass body and 1000 lb (454 kg) payload capacity. Top speed is 53 mph (85.3 km/hr); range is 95 miles (152 km) at a constant 40 mph (64 km/hr) at full payload.

Vehicle curb weight is 5,100 lbs (2,312 kg), of which 2,340 lbs (1,064 kg) is lead-acid batteries. The vehicle manufacturer is Antares Engineering.

Battronic Minivan

The Battronic Truck Company, a division of Boyertown Auto Body Works, Boyertown, Pa., U.S.A., has produced the Minivan in conjunction with the Electric Vehicle Council (EVC).

The EVC is a non-profit association dedicated to the proliferation of electric power for transportation. Its membership includes electric power producers, manufacturers of related products, university members, and individuals involved in government and research organizations in nineteen countries throughout the world.

One of the EVC functions is the development of a vehicle which could demonstrate the effectiveness of electric transportation. The Battronic Minivan, a 1/4-ton (227 kg) battery-operated truck, was produced and distributed to 64 U.S. utilities in 32 states. A total of 110 Minivans have accumulated over 100,000 aggregate miles (160,934 km) of on-road experience. The EVC is using this demonstration to gather and tabulate data for research purposes.

The specifications of the Minivan include: an electronic SCR controller, series-wound 112-volt motor and a patented quick-change battery system. Maximum vehicle weight with load is 6,800 lbs (3084 kg); top speed is about 60 mph (97 km/hr).

Photo courtesy of Lead Industries Association/Battronic, Inc.

The QT uses an 8.5 hp motor which provides a top speed of 30 mph (48 km/hr) in 30 seconds. Range from the 860 lb (390 kg) battery pack is 30 miles (48 km). Total vehicle weight is 3,300 lbs (1496 kg).

Jet Industries Electra-Van

One outstanding new electric vehicle design is the Electra-Van from Jet Industries, Austin, Texas. This 2,350 lb (1060 kg) light utility/pleasure 5-door van carries 960 lbs (435 kg) of lead-acid batteries. The 15-hp 3800-rpm DC traction motor uses a solid-state controller and a 4-speed transaxle.

Top speed is 55 mph (88 km/hr); acceleration is zero to 30 mph (48 km/hr) in 9 seconds. Cruising speed is 38 mph (61 km/hr) and range is 60 to 100 miles (96 to 161 km). The gross vehicle weight of the Electra-Van is 3,250 lbs (1470 kg). For more information contact: Jet Industries, 4201 South Congress, Austin, Texas U.S.A.

Photo courtesy of General Electric Corp.

The QT Electric Utility Van

The experimental QT (Quiet Truck) is a joint development of General Electric Transportation Systems and the International Lead Zinc Research Organization, Inc.

ELECTRA-VAN

ELECTRA-VAN
ASSEMBLY LINE

Photos courtesy of EVA Corp.

The EVA ElectroVan

The Electric Vehicle Associates of Cleveland, Ohio, have a prototype design for inner-city delivery and shuttle vans. Each van can handle a 500-pound (227-kg) payload with a range of 40 miles (64 km) per charge. A 96-volt 200-amp-hour battery pack is exchanged through side access doors. Duties of the EVA ElectroVan include light hauling, personnel carrying and postal service. For more information write EVA, 9100 Bank St., Cleveland, Ohio 44125.

TITAN

MINUTE MISER

Photos courtesy of Cushman OMC

EXECUTIVE

Cushman—OMC

The Cushman Division of the Outboard Marine Corporation of Lincoln, Nebraska, U.S.A. produces three electric utility vehicles.

The electric 2-passenger "Minute Miser" is designed for in-plant commercial use. Top speed is 11 mph (18km/hr), range is 35 miles (56 km) per charge. The 24-volt system uses four deep-cycle 6-volt batteries and a 2.7 to 4.3 hp motor. Vehicle weight is 650 lbs (295 kg).

The "Executive" model has a 500-lb (227-kg) carrying capacity and an 11-mph (18-km/hr) top speed with optional motor. A 36-volt system uses a 5 hp maximum power DC series-wound motor. Thousands of these units are in service performing functions in security, VIP and plant duties. An optional cab is available for outdoor use.

The "Titan" model features two versions, the "316" and the "318." The "316" has a 13 mph (21 km/hr) top speed, 35 mile range (56 km) and maximum 2,000 lb (907 kg) load capacity. The "318" model has a 48-volt battery supply, range of 28 miles per charge (45 km) and top speed of 20 mph (32 km/hr). This heavy-duty vehicle is also available in an enclosed cab version.

For more information, write: CUSHMAN-OMC, P.O. Box 82409, Lincoln, Nebraska, 68501, U.S.A.

Photo courtesy of White Motor Corp.

A HYSTER B 60 BL "WALKIE RIDER"

Photos courtesy of Hyster Company Industrial Truck Operations

The Electric Forklift

A number of companies designed electric forklifts during the thirties. The early models used resistance controllers to vary speeds, which was inefficient. Today, modern forklifts use solid-state controllers—a major step enabling electrics to compete with their internal combustion counterparts handling loads of up to 10,000 lbs (4535 kg).

Certain jobs are ideally suited to electrics, which can quietly and safely operate indoors to perform both conventional forklift chores as well as highly specialized duty. The use of the electric industrial truck is now extensive throughout the world. The inherent design of the forklift, which is required to carry heavy ballast weight to balance loads, lends itself well to carrying batteries. This is one of the few examples of using battery weight as a design advantage.

A NARROW AISLE HYSTER ELECTRIC REACH TRUCK

Photo courtesy of Hyster Company Industrial Truck Operations

DEVELOPMENT IN ENGLAND

LUCAS ELECTRIC LIMOUSINE

Lucas Batteries, Limited

One of the leading British electric vehicle manufacturers is Lucas Batteries, Ltd., of Birmingham, England. Efforts made by Lucas have created additional markets for their batteries and electric vehicle components.

The Lucas Electric Taxi is a result of strong product development in a vehicle designed for a specific purpose. The side-entry battery exchange system allows for rapid exchange. It has been designed to operate in a typical London cab working cycle.

The first Lucas Electric Taxi was demonstrated to the public at the London Motor Show in October, 1975. The result of additional studies led to the production of two prototype Mark III Electric Taxis. The controller used was a solid-state SCR type, incorporating regenerative braking. The projected range is 70 miles (112 km) to 140 miles (224 km) at a constant 30 mph (48 km/hr). The maximum speed of the vehicle is over 50 mph (80 km/hr) with acceleration of zero to 30 miles per hour (0 to 48 km/hr) in 14 seconds fully laden. Thirty-six lightweight 6-volt lead-acid traction batteries power a 216-volt DC, 37-kw (50 bhp) series-wound, 4,600 RPM motor.

The Lucas Electric Midi-Bus has a top speed of 50 miles per hour (80 km/hr) with a low speed range of about 112 miles (180 km) without passengers. The Midi-Bus has been in service between Birmingham and Manchester, England, a 40-mile (64-km) circuit, since early 1975.

The Lucas Electric Delivery Van/Personnel Carrier has demonstrated a variety of services

LUCAS ELECTRIC TAXI

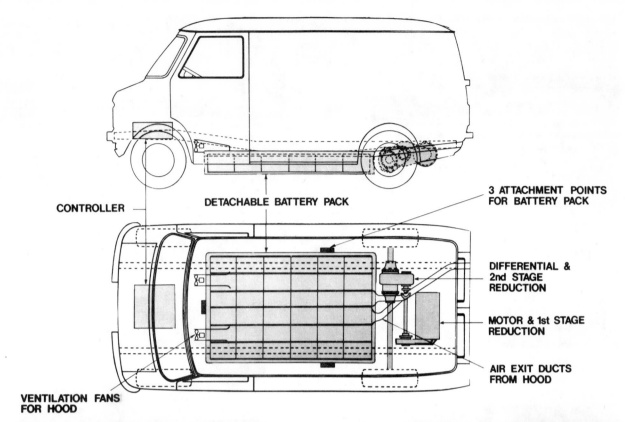

CONTROLLER

DETACHABLE BATTERY PACK

3 ATTACHMENT POINTS FOR BATTERY PACK

DIFFERENTIAL & 2nd STAGE REDUCTION

MOTOR & 1st STAGE REDUCTION

AIR EXIT DUCTS FROM HOOD

VENTILATION FANS FOR HOOD

LUCAS CF ELECTRIC VANS AND TRUCKS   All Photos courtesy of Special Projects Division, Lucas Batteries Ltd., Birmingham, England

for fleet operators, including the post office. It has a one-ton payload (907 kg) and can accommodate up to nine people plus the driver with space for luggage. The passenger-carrying version is called the Lucas Electric Pullman, designed for airport-to-hotel use; the non-passenger variety is called the Lucas Electric Delivery Van.

Two other variations of the delivery van are the Lucas Electric Limousine and the Lucas Electric Crew Bus, which are dome-roofed vehicles designed for passenger comfort and ease of entry. Again, the battery pack has been designed for quick battery exchanges. The range for these models is 70 miles (113 km) per charge minimum and up to 140 miles (225 km) at 30 mph (48 km/hr) with a top speed of 50 mph (80 km/hr).

The Lucas Company believes this type of vehicle is ideal for use in areas where internal combustion vehicles are forbidden, such as inside food warehouses, supermarkets, postal sorting offices and hospitals.

TROPICANA

Photos courtesy Electration, Ltd.

PRECINCT

RICKSHAW

ElecTraction Ltd.

THE TROPICANA: the ElecTraction ''Tropicana'' is a two/three-passenger leisure sports car which shares its running chassis with four other special purpose vehicles: the ''Rickshaw,'' ''Bermuda,'' ''Precinct,'' and ''Campus'' models.

The bodies are corrosion-free, reinforced plastic. All mechanical and electrical components are standard off-the-shelf production items which have proven themselves in automotive and industrial truck use.

All use the chassis of the ElecTraction E700 Electric Truck, which is designed for industrial duties and light delivery.

THE PRECINCT: the Precinct is a two-door coupe that can be adapted to a variety of sizes and duties, including a vehicle for disabled persons.

THE RICKSHAW: the Rickshaw is a four-seater, available with or without doors and equipped with a variety of weather protection options.

Twelve 6-volt 151-amp/hr lead-acid batteries are carried in two packs of six, weighing a total of 720 pounds (326 kg). The total curb weight of the vehicle, including batteries, is 1,600 pounds (726 kg), and the laden weight is 2,200 pounds (997 kg).

TRUSTY TRUCK

Photos courtesy of Electration, Ltd.

E700 TRUCK AND TRUSTY-TRUCK: the chassis features 14-gauge tubular steel construction, with a 7.5 hp motor and thyristor controller. Performance is a 50-to-60 mile (80 to 96 km) range at speeds of up to 35 mph (56 km/hr). The heavy-duty traction battery pack is rated at 72-volts and produced by the Oldham Company, one of Britain's largest battery makers.

For further information, write ElecTraction, Heybridge Basin, Maldon, Essex, England.

Silent Karrier

The Silent-Karrier is a two-ton delivery van designed to handle a payload of 3,500 lbs (1587 kg). The vehicle is produced by the Chloride Group, Ltd., of London, England, and was developed jointly by Chloride, Chrysler of the United Kingdom, and The National Freight Corporation. The Silent Karrier has a range of 40 miles (64 km) per charge.

Photo courtesy of Lead Industries Association/Chloride

E700 TRUCK

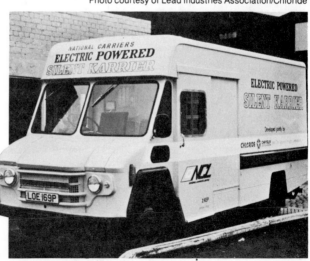

SILENT KARRIER

Photo courtesy of the Electric Vehicle News

The Milk Float

The United Kingdom has a population of over 56 million people. Each person drinks about five pints of milk per week.

This little tidbit of information may, at first glance, seem irrelevant, except that the United Kingdom operates a force of about 50,000 electric vehicles to deliver the milk to British inhabitants. The home delivery of milk and dairy products is unique to Great Britain, hence the existence of the "milk float."

The milk float averages abut 300 miles (483 km) per week of quiet, non-polluting duty. It makes one wonder why a similar application of multi-stop service has not been applied to a greater degree in other countries.

The British maintain that a reduction in pollution is merely a side effect or bonus derived from these vehicles, and that the major motivation is the economy and excellent service record which accompanies this type of delivery method. Economy allows this type of delivery service to exist in the first place, because if in-

ternal combustion vehicles at a higher price had to be used, the service would be endangered. Records of dependability from this form of mulit-stop-and-start transportation have been remarkable. And, although the initial cost of the electric milk float is high, the lower running costs easily outstrip the difference in purchase price.

With over fifteen million miles (24 million km) per year spent delivering over two hundred million tons (180 billion kg) of milk and dairy products, traveling more than forty miles (64 km) per day, while making up to 250 starts and stops daily, the British electric milk float is a credit to any commercial enterprise.

Residual benefits, such as quietness of operation, pollution-free service, and absolute dependability make one wonder why the use of electric vehicles for mail delivery and short-haul operations has not proliferated more rapidly in an energy-sensitive world.

HYBRID TAXI

AMBULANCE

DEVELOPMENT IN ITALY

Progetti Gestioni Ecologiche, an Italian firm, has designed a computerized rental system with recharging stations for city residents. This system was conceived to complement their production electric vehicle designs.

Their prototypes include a ten-passenger school bus, which weighs 2,734 lbs (1,240 kg) and can carry ten pupils plus a driver for a distance of 62 miles (100 km) urban and 87 miles (140 km) highway at 28 mph (45 km/hr). Top speed is 37 mph (60 km/hr).

The PGE ambulance is basically the same vehicle. This three-passenger automobile weighs 1,653 lbs (750 kg) and uses a 72-volt motor, producing a top speed of 37 mph (60 km/hr) and a range of 47 miles (75 km) urban and 68 miles (110 km) highway at 31 mph (50 km/hr).

The PGE Hybrid Taxi is basically the same external vehicle size as the ambulance and school bus, but weighs 3,197 lbs (1,450 kg) and is designed to carry a driver and four passengers with luggage. The 72-volt electric motor yields speeds of 37 mph (60 km/hr). The internal-combustion engine can yield 130 km/hr. Range is 62 miles (100 km) for urban and 87 miles (140 km) for highway driving at 28 mph (45 km/hr).

Other PGE vehicles include a hybrid van and six-passenger personnel carrier, plus a larger 3,638 lbs (1,650 kg) van which can carry 1,763 lbs (800 kg). Controls are solid state with thyristors and regenerative braking. Acceleration for the van is zero to 19 mph (30 km/hr) in six seconds.

Part of the PGE concept is a vehicle fleet hiring system to be used for town dwellers. This system is keyed into a credit card and computer. The renter picks up his vehicle at a charging station and returns it at another station, plugs in and leaves. PGE already has one prototype rental station located in Padua, Italy. Customers there are reported very satisfied with the computerized system.

Photo courtesy of Lead Industries Association/FIAT

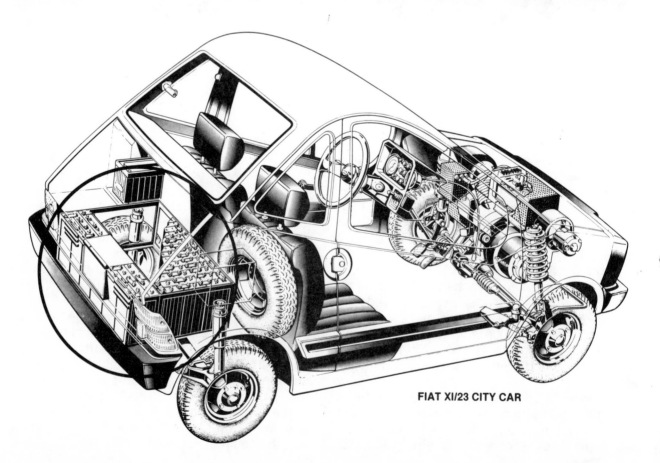

FIAT XI/23 CITY CAR

Fiat XI/23 City Car

The Fiat XI/23 is a two-seat passenger car with a maximum speed of 47 mph (75 km/hr) and a range of 45 miles (70 km) at a constant 31 mph (50 km/hr).

This prototype city car features front-wheel drive, a 13.5 hp DC motor, with separate excitation, and a transistorized solid-state controller with regenerative braking.

The most significant advance is the use of Yardney nickel-zinc batteries which have a maximum capacity 1.75 times that of conventional lead-acid batteries.

Curb weight is 1810 lbs (820 kg), of which 370 lbs (166 kg) is batteries.

Zagato

The Zagato Zele 1000, Zele 2000, and Zele Van are produced in Italy by Zagato, the famous coach builder.

The 1000 and 2000 models are both two-door sport coupes, while the van is a three-door model which is 10″ (25 cm) longer to provide cargo space. All models have fiberglass bodies and weigh between 1,091 lbs (495 kg) and 1,378 lbs (625 kg), depending upon battery selection.

Traction batteries provide power to the 6 hp DC electric motor while a 12-volt SLI battery operates accessories.

Top speed varies from 25 to 40 mph (40 to 65 km/hr), depending upon model. Range per charge is 31 to 40 miles (50 to 65 km).

This vehicle has been marketed in the U.S. under the name Elcar. Marketing plans for Elcar inlcude a model called the Wagonette, an extended version weighing 1,500 lbs (680 kg).

Other Italian efforts have been centered around ENEL, the Italian electric utility. ENEL has sponsored an electric vehicle development program with Fiat since late 1973. Two Fiat 850-T models were used to demonstrate the difference between shunt and series DC motors.

Another Italian electric is a three-wheeled vehicle based on the Vespa car. Also, an electric car researched and developed by Gianni Roglianni and designed by Giovanni Michelotti was introduced in Turin in 1974. This small 1,100 lb (500 kg) city car has a top speed of 37 mph (58 km/hr) and a range of 30 miles (48 km) per charge, using a 4 hp motor. Both the chassis and the body are primarily aluminum.

ZAGATO/ELCAR

Photo courtesy of Lead Industries Association/Zagato

DEVELOPMENT IN CANADA

Marathon C-300

The Marathon C-300 is a 2-passenger production electric automobile with a fiberglass body and canvas top. The 2300 lb (1043 kg) vehicle has a 500 lb (227 kg) payload capacity. Operating range is 50 miles (80 km) with a cruising speed of 35 mph (56 km/hr). Twelve 6-volt deep-cycle heavy-duty batteries are stored behind the passenger compartment. The 72-volt 8-hp DC motor and variable-speed standard transmission are located under the front hood.

The Marathon is available in "high profile" and "low profile" models from Marathon Electric Cars, Ltd., 8305 Le Creusot, Ville De St. Leonard, Quebec HIP 2A2 Canada.

DEVELOPMENT IN HOLLAND

The Witkar System

The Witkar "White Car" System, established in 1974, is an Amsterdam, Holland-based electric rental Cooperative Association with 3,000 members. Thirty five three-wheeled, 860 lb (390 kg) two-passenger 20-mph (32-km/hr) cars with polyester resin bodies are powered by nickel-cadmium batteries which recharge in minutes at five stations located throughout the central Amsterdam area.

A member inserts a magnetically-coded key into a station terminal, selects his destination and uses the first car in line. Members pay a one-time fee of 50 guilders ($20) for their card and a rental fee of one guilder (40 cents) for 10 minutes of use.

The Witkar System was conceived by Luud Schimmelpennink, now secretary of the Association, who plans to expand operations to 15 stations and 100 cars.

Photo courtesy of Lead Industries Association

DEVELOPMENT IN GERMANY

Electric vehicle development in Germany is a joint effort by automobile, battery, electrical, and heavy machine industries under the coordination of the GES (Gesell-Schaft Fur Electrischen Strassenzerkehr mbh, Dusseldorf), a subsidiary of RWE, the country's largest electric utility.

GES acts as a clearinghouse for development by component and vehicle manufacturers. Therefore, integration of mutually beneficial technology into all areas of the cooperative is realized.

A total of 20 MAN buses are experimentally servicing three public lines on a full schedule basis in Dusseldorf and nearby Monchenglad-bach. The MAN Electrobus Program is partially subsidized by the government. In October, 1974, in Monchengladbach, seven electric buses replaced diesels on a 25 mile (40 km) round trip with 88 stops between the city's center and a nearby town. A range of 50 miles (80 km) per battery charge was possible from each bus. Battery exchange takes only about five minutes, easily comparable to refueling a conventional diesel bus.

Mercedes-Benz hybrid electric buses will also be used in a similar program. Another GES test involved 20 Volkswagen and 30 Mercedes-Benz Electric Vans, with an additional 80 vehicles to be added at a later date.

Photo courtesy of Messerschmitt-Bolkow-Blohm

MBB Electro-Transporter

An electric transport vehicle has been developed by MBB (Messerschmitt-Bolkow-Blohm) in Germany. MBB collaborated with Bosch for electric propulsion, Varta for batteries, and Bayer Chemicals for the self-supporting plastic chassis.

Gross vehicle weight is 7,275 lbs (3,300 kg); payload is 2,205 lbs (1,000 kg); battery weight is 1,918 lbs (870 kg).

Features include a 60 hp motor, a maximum vehicle speed of 50 mph (80 km/hr), and range of 37 to 65 miles (60 to 105 km).

The chassis can accommodate eight different body styles from a flatbed truck to a small bus. Plastic body construction allows current-carrying connections to be embedded in plastic.

MAN ELECTRIC BUS

Photo courtesy of Volkswagenwerk AG

MERCEDES-BENZ HYBRID-ELECTRIC BUS

Photo courtesy of Volkswagenwerk AG

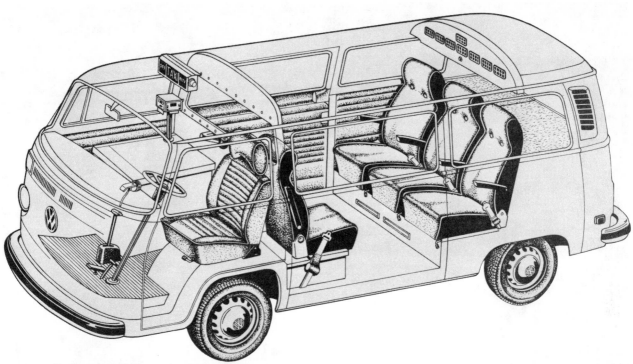

THE VOLKSWAGEN HYBRID-ELECTRIC CITY TAXI
Features include a bulletproof glass and steel wall which separates driver from passengers, and automatic electrically controlled right-side access door.

Photo courtesy of Volkswagenwerk AG

The Volkswagen Company, responding to the need for a city taxi, has produced a hybrid gasoline-electric model, based on the Microbus. This vehicle was specifically designed to be used as a taxi, including such considerations as special seats which carry up to four adults with room for luggage, a wheelchair, or baby carriage. Volkswagen considers this vehicle the taxi of the future.

The hybrid taxi uses a 50-DIN horsepower, 1600-CC gasoline engine and a Bosch DC shunt motor. In the electric mode, the vehicle achieves a maximum speed of 43.5 mph (70 km/hr). The hybrid mode produces a maximum speed of 64.6 mph (104 km/hr) and acceleration of zero to 62 mph (100 km/hr) in 31 seconds. The overall operating range is comparable to a conventional internal combustion engined vehicle; fuel consumption is 20 mpg (8.5 km/L).

In "hybrid" operation the vehicle's driving power comes from a combination of both the electric motor and gasoline engine. The vehicle starts out on electric power provided by eleven storage batteries, then switches to the gasoline engine at higher speeds. In cases where the gasoline engine cannot produce enough power

to meet the vehicle's needs, the electric motor automatically resumes support, with both power systems used to propel the vehicle.

If the gasoline engine produces more power than needed at any time, the electric motor, acting as a generator, is used to recharge the batteries.

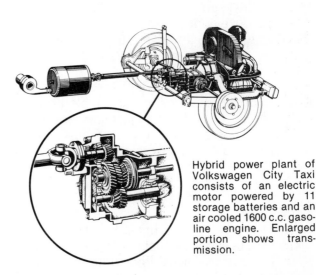

Hybrid power plant of Volkswagen City Taxi consists of an electric motor powered by 11 storage batteries and an air cooled 1600 c.c. gasoline engine. Enlarged portion shows transmission.

(LEFT) MERCEDES-BENZ ELECTRIC VAN (RIGHT) VOLKSWAGEN COMMERCIAL

Photo courtesy of Volkswagenwerk AG

A recent announcement from Volkswagenwerk AG indicated the production of an all-electric Volkswagen Commercial. The vehicle uses a 33-kw (44-bhp) motor with a continuous output of about 14 kw (22 bhp). Acceleration is zero to 31 mph (50 km/hr) in 12 seconds with a maximum speed of 44 mph (70 km/hr). A thyristor is used to control the energy from the 1896 lb (860 kg) battery pack, with a 144-volt, 180-amp-hour capacity. The Commercial has a range of 31 to 50 miles (50 to 80 km) on a single charge.

Actual development of the Volkswagen Electric Commercial started in 1969. Since 1972, experimental vehicles such as the Elektro Transporter have covered more than 310,000 miles (500,000 km) in service. The Volkswagen Electric Commercial will be assembled on the same production line as the gasoline version.

Prior to the announcement of Volkswagen production plans, tests were conducted by GES and Lufthansa German Airlines which aided in the accumulation of data on several GES-test bed vehicles, including a Mercedes-Benz Electric Van.

Volkswagen and GES mutually developed an electric passenger car using the chassis of an Audi 100. A new nickel-iron battery by Varta powered the experimental vehicle. Besides serving as a test bed for the new nickel-iron batteries, attention was also given to a new motor and a combination of hydraulic torque converter and electronic control system utilizing field weakening.

Germany considers the possibility of 20% electric vehicles by the year 2000. German designers say ten more years of research and development will be necessary to perfect a total electric infrastructure of vehicles, service, and electric power production.

Photo courtesy of Volkswagenwerk AG

The Elektro-Transporter or Volkswagen Commercial, showing side-loading battery access tray.

DEVELOPMENT IN JAPAN

In the future, Japan may capture a large share of the American electric vehicle market. Reports indicate that current Japanese electric vehicle progress leads the efforts of all nations, including the U.S. Japan is a country where the small automobile is an accepted fact and pollution is at a dangerous level. The Japanese began funding their electric vehicle program in 1971.

Japan is the world's largest importer of oil, which further motivates them to accelerate development of electric vehicles. It is to their advantage to have worldwide oil consumption decreased. The electric vehicle is the cornerstone of that program.

A cooperative effort, between the Japanese government and private companies contributes to the solution of technological problems. They have produced sophisticated prototypes which incorporate styling, sales appeal, and the latest technology. The Japan Electric Vehicle Association organized in 1976 is composed of manufacturers of vehicles and components and includes such companies as Toyota, Nissan, and Mitsubishi. The development program includes electric passenger cars, trucks, and buses. New batteries are being studied, along with components, electronic control devices, and motors. The result of this data has produced four types of lightweight and compact electric cars and trucks. In the first phase of this program, three vehicles were constructed with advanced lead-acid batteries. Seven types of lead-acid batteries, plus others using materials such as zinc, were also produced. In 1976, four second-phase experimental vehicles began demonstration tests in city and suburban operation. The vehicles ran a total distance of 1,864 miles (3000 km) averaging 50 to 62 miles (80 to 100 km) per day on flat and hilly terrain.

The Daihatsu, Mitsubishi, Toyota, and Toyo Kogyo Companies have been involved in developing ten different types of electric vans and trucks. In addition, ten types of electric vehicles have been fabricated since 1967 by Japanese electric utility companies for demonstration purposes. These have been basically gasoline vehicles converted to electric power. Demonstrations directed at newspaper delivery, milk delivery and service-oriented vehicles for power companies have been stressed. There are twelve electric buses in operation in large Japanese cities to date.

Mazda Titan Hybrid Truck

This vehicle uses both diesel and electric power in combination. The DC electric motor uses series-parallel switching controls with four 12 v lead-acid batteries. The 2,977 cc diesel engine can power the 5115 lb (2,320 kg) truck at speeds of up to 62 mph (100 km/hr) with a range of 6.2 miles (10 km). Batteries are automatically recharged while driven under diesel power.

Photo courtesy of Toyo Kogyo Co., Ltd.

Toyota EV-2

The EV-2 is a second-stage experimental electric automobile developed in cooperation with the Japanese government. The vehicle was designed for use in metropolitan areas similar to Japanese cities. These parameters include special attention to extended range and acceleration rather than high speed and the ability to climb grades. Speed limits in Japan are 25 mph (40 km/hr).

The four-passenger body is designed to be ultra-lightweight yet strong by incorporating curved surfaces and reinforced ribs for maximum strength. Total vehicle weight is 2,767 lbs (1255 kg). The 1169 lb (530 kg) hybrid battery pack consists of a high-energy-density zinc-air battery for range and an advanced lead-acid battery for power. A separately excited DC motor rated at 20-38 kilowatts powers the rear wheels through a two-speed automatic transmission and a solid-state controller.

Photo courtesy of Lead Industries Association/Toyota

Maximum speed is 53 mph (85 km/hr); range is 283 miles (455 km) at a constant 25 mph (40 km/hr) and 155 miles (250 km) in a stop-and-go driving cycle. Acceleration is 0 to 25 mph (40 km/hr) in 6 seconds.

Nissan EV-4

Nissan Motor Company, manufacturer of Datsun motorcars, developed in cooperation with the Japanese government two experimental vehicles named EV-4.

The first vehicle, EV-4-P, is claimed to have the highest range of any electric vehicle powered by a lead-acid battery system. The range at 25 mph (40 km/hr) for the compact truck is 188 miles (302 km). Top speed is 54 mph (87 km/hr); acceleration is 0 to 25 mph (0 to 40 km/hr) in 6.9 seconds.

A 27-kw shunt-wound DC motor is controlled through a SCR chopper.

The second model, EV-4-H, is claimed to have the highest range of any electric vehicle. The compact truck uses a hybrid battery system of a zinc-air and lead-acid battery in combination. Range at 25 mph (40 km/hr) is 308 miles (496 km). Top speed is 56 mph (90 km/hr) and acceleration is 0-25 mph (0-40 km/hr) in 4.9 seconds. The EV-4-H uses a 20-kw shunt-wound DC motor controlled through an SCR chopper with provision for regenerative braking. Total efficiency from battery to motor is 78%. The two-passenger truck construction relies heavily on fiber-reinforced plastic and aluminum. Vehicle weight is 5,490 lbs (2,490 kg). A special design consideration allows for easy battery exchange through a side-loading tray arrangement.

Photo courtesy of Nissan Motor Company

Photo courtesy Nissan Motor Company

Nissan Laurel

Two Japanese electric passenger cars were produced by Nissan in 1974. A Datsun 200L and a Nissan Laurel were developed to be used by VIPs at the International Oceanographic Exposition in Okinawa, 1975.

Designed for short trips, the five-passenger vehicles had a range of 40 miles (65 km). Top speed was 53 mph (85 km/hr). Features included air conditioning, power brakes, thyristor, and 2-speed automatic transmission. Total vehicle weight was 4,230 lbs (1919 kg.)

Photo courtesy of the Electric Vehicle News/Daihatsu

Daihatsu

This four passenger lightweight automobile prototype has a maximum speed of 55 mph (89 km/hr) and a range of 109 miles (175 km) per charge, at a constant 25 mph (40 km/hr). This vehicle can accelerate from 0 to 19 mph (30 km/hr) in 2.4 seconds. Gross vehicle weight is 2500 lbs. (1132 kg).

Toyo Kogyo

The Toyo Kogyo Company is one of Japan's largest vehicle manufacturers. Since 1966 several Mazda electric vehicles have been developed under an agency of the Ministry of International Trade and Industry (MITI).

One vehicle, the Ev3 Phase II, has a 127 mile (205 km) range at 25 mph (40 km/hr). This model, (not shown) is a lightweight flat bed truck weighing 1716 lbs (778 kg). Top speed is 45 mph (72 km/hr).

MAZDA BONGO VAN

Photo courtesy Toyo Kogyo Co., Ltd.

Mazda Bongo Van

This 5-seater minibus weighs 2,789 lbs. (1,265 kg). Top speed is 40 mph (65 km/hr), range is 37 miles (60 km) per charge. Vehicle weight is 2,789 lbs (1,265 kg). A 4-speed transmission is used. Eight 12 v lead-acid batteries supply power to the 19.2 kw DC motor.

Mazda Familia Passenger Car

The Familia is a four passenger automobile weighing 2424 lbs (1100 kg). Eight 12 v advanced lead-acid batteries provide power to the 11 km DC motor via a Thyristor chopper. Top speed is more than 50 mph (80 km/hr). Range is more than 44 miles (70 km) per charge.

MAZDA FAMILIA PASSENGER CAR

Photo courtesy Toyo Kogyo Co., Ltd.

ELECTRIC TAXI CABS

The next time you ride in a taxicab in a heavily-populated metropolitan area, notice two things: one, that the vehicle is moving very slowly and two, that the pollution level is usually quite high. You will observe long lines of taxi cabs waiting at taxi stands, idling their engines adding to the pollution level, and you'll see a great number of empty taxi cabs cruising for a fare. There is a need for a better system. In areas such as Chicago, for example, where the pollution concentrations are now higher than EPA standards, city governments should institute a plan which would incorporate electric taxicabs into their transportation grid.

The Lucas Electric Taxi, made in Britain, and the GES Hybrid Electric Volkswagen Microbus used as a taxi are two examples of the feasibility of electric vehicles using current state-of-the-art battery technology.

Surely, vehicles such as these could be assimilated into a large city's taxicab network. Perhaps the governing body of a metropolitan area should regulate the percentage of gasoline-powered taxicabs allowed within the highly congested areas. The balance of these vehicles could be electric-powered or electric hybrids. A map displayed on the taxi would tell the customer that the vehicle is electric and that trips would be limited to a five mile radius. Such a taxi would stay within the heavily-populated

PGE HYBRID TAXI

area, thereby reducing emissions in congested neighborhoods. The cab driver would benefit because short trips are profitable in tips; on short trip fares he receives more money per mile (km) and hour of driving. He could also be compensated with an incentive bonus for driving the electric. The money for this bonus could come out of the saving the taxi company would realize due to lower maintenance and replacement costs.

State-of-the-art batteries would start this program off, but as newer battery systems are developed and replace the old, the range and usable hours of operation could be increased.

The production of vehicles designed to be

LUCAS ELECTRIC TAXI

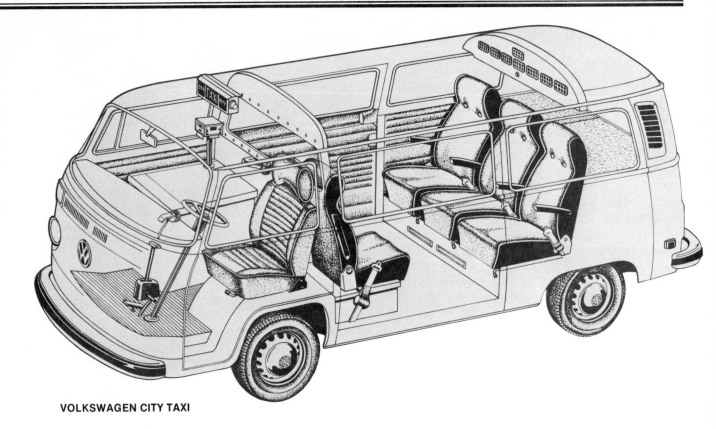

VOLKSWAGEN CITY TAXI

taxicabs will result in maximizing passenger and driver creature comforts. Provisions for carrying luggage would be needed because, although the electric taxi would not go to airports — bus, train terminals and hotels would be served. For city use, the electric taxi would never have to exceed 40 mph (64 km/hr) which is within today's technology. Materials could be plastic or rubber. After all, a rubber fender would never rust and could be bumped many times without ever leaving a dent. The use of hydrogen and oxygen fuel cells would be feasible because the number of cells that could be purchased for a fleet of taxicabs would rate a cost-saving quantity price. Then too, the heat required for winter operation could be converted directly from the hydrogen in a combustion-type catalytic heater.

An urban electric taxicab could be integrated into our system today. This is not beyond our technical capabilities. Hopefully, it is not beyond our political capabilities, because of the red tape necessary to implement such a system. Inhabitants and workers in congested areas must spend many hours a day in an atmosphere that is polluted beyond acceptable standards. An electric taxi would benefit these people in more ways than providing convenient clean transportation.

ELECTRIC MASS TRANSPORTATION

When the early railroad ran through an area, a city would sprout up as a natural consequence. The railroad industry was not merely a means of transportation, but literally an architect of the land.

Today, the relatively slow speeds of trains, due to equipment limitations and track deficiencies, seriously impair the value of the railroad as a passenger mode of transportation. The cost of maintaining a safe and clean right of way for a railroad is high, but insignificant compared with the cost of constructing a new rail system from scratch in today's economy. Also safety considerations must be made for passenger trains capable of traveling at speeds of 125 mph (200 km/hr) or more on existing tracks.

Today, there are many areas where high speed trains would not be feasible due to poor track conditions. A solution to the track problem must be reached or the railroad may be relegated to freight service.

Perhaps the railroads could benefit more from government participation. This is not to say that the government would own the railroads, but the road beds could be nationalized, thereby allowing them to be rebuilt and electrified. This process would convert the diesel-electric locomotives into pure electrics. As the electrification system progresses, the diesel-electric would run on total electric power more frequently.

This undertaking would be extremely expensive by any standard of economics. But, it would enable freight and passenger service to be powered electrically—from coal, nuclear, or other generation methods. This would allow the railroad industry to again become a valuable asset.

When one considers that it requires seven years from inception through research, development, and production to build an automobile from scratch, we can imagine how long it would take to modernize any significant portion of our rail system. Therefore this is a project that must be started immediately to bear fruit in 20 years.

For short-trip passenger use, perhaps new tracks can be installed in certain areas, but an entire revamping would be required to produce trains that can travel 500 mph, which is possible in the distant future. In the future transportation grid, more emphasis will be put on mass transportation because it can utilize electricity to its utmost potential. The concept of linear induction vehicles makes possible a mode of transportation that could certainly be called space age travel.

The idea for the linear induction device was suggested in 1895. The thought of transportation from one place to another without the use of wheels is certainly older than any other method of getting about. Remember that all animals, birds, fish, and insects do a pretty good job of getting from one place to another without wheels. Sail boats, surfboards, ice skates, skis, and gliders are also examples of this method or transportation. The millipede is an insect that travels with the wave action of its legs, which is basically what happens in a linear induction device which travels on a wave of magnetic force. The linear induction motor has no moving parts. The vehicle is literally pushed along a monorail track or through a tunnel floating on magnetic cushions that provide friction-less travel. Prototype models have been developed by companies such as Messerschmitt-Bol-kow-Blohm and Krauss-Maffei of Germany to prove that this type of vehicle is feasible.

Just when we will see linear induction vehicles on a wide scale will depend on many economic factors; however, when this mode becomes a reality, we will see less reliance upon air travel for short city-to-city commuter use.

MODERN RAPID TRANSIT
Boeing Rapid Transit cars service ground level, elevated and subway lines in Chicago, Illinois. Electric-train mass transportation has been in operation here since 1895.

Photo courtesy of Boeing-Vertol Company

Transrapid—EMS

TRANSRAPID—EMS is a joint venture of two German companies, Messerschmitt-Bolkow—Blohm (MBB) and Krauss-Maffei. Their individual research and development since the late 1960's was combined in 1974 to produce high-speed ground transportation systems. The core of this technology is centered around magnetically-levitated, LIV's (Linear Induction Vehicles).

Photo courtesy of Transrapid—EMS (Krauss-Maffei & MBB)

BASIC VEHICLE

A basic test vehicle was demonstrated to the public in May, 1971, by MBB. This experiment proved the technical feasibility of a large-scale magnetically-elevated LIV. A speed of 56 mph (90.km/hr) was achieved on a 2,165-foot (660-m) straight test track by the 12,787 lb (5,800 kg) vehicle.

Photo courtesy of Transrapid—EMS (Krauss-Maffei & MBB)

TRANSRAPID 02

In October, 1971, Krauss-Maffei demonstrated to the public an 11-ton (11,300-kg) magnetically-elevated LIV with a maximum speed of 102 mph (164 km/hr).

TRANSRAPID 03

Comparison trials between magnetically-levitated vehicles and air-cushion vehicles were made by using the TRANSRAPID 03, an air-cushion 87-mph (140-km/hr) LIV weighing 21,164 lbs (9,600 kg). Results of the tests proved the superiority of magnetic levitation, thereby halting air-cushion technology development.

TRANSRAPID 04

TRANSRAPID 04 is the largest magnetically-levitated experimental passenger-carrying LIV in existence to date. A 7,874-ft (2,400-m) elevated test track is used to test components under realistic conditions and at higher speeds. The result of these tests is the basis for LIV research and development. The TRANSRAPID 04 has a weight of 40,786 lbs (18,500 kg) and a top speed of 155 mph (250 km/hr). Future vehicles with top speeds of up to 311 mph (500 km/hr) are anticipated.

TRANSRAPID 03 Photo courtesy of Transrapid—EMS
(Krauss-Maffei & MBB)

TRANSRAPID 04 Photo courtesy of Transrapid—EMS (Krauss-Maffei & MBB)

DEMAG & MBB Cabinlift

Two German companies, DEMAG and MBB, have developed a variety of systems incorporating the monorail concept. The Cabinlift is designed as a low-cost alternative to traffic tunnels linking office, industrial, hospital, and airport buildings.

The vehicles travel on rubber tires and use linear induction motors. Heated cabs vary in carrying capacity from 6 to 25 persons, and are totally automated.

Morgantown PRT System

Boeing Personal Rapid Transit (PRT) cars travel between two campuses of West Virginia University at Morgantown. The PRT system is a fleet of driverless rubber-tired vehicles which operate under fully automated computer control on 5.3 miles (8.5 km) of concrete guideway at a cruising speed of 30 mph (48.3 km/hr). Each vehicle uses a 70-hp compound-wound DC motor. The system was developed by Boeing Aerospace Company as a national demonstration project for the U.S. Department of Transportation's Urban Mass Transportation Administration. It is operated by West Virginia University with Boeing assistance. The Morgantown system is the only automated people mover currently in operation in an urban setting. It has carried four

DEMAG & MBB CABINLIFT   Photo courtesy of
Cabinlift DEMAG & MBB

million passengers since October, 1975. Forty five vehicles are presently employed; however, new plans include an expanded system with 28 additional cars.

MORGANTOWN PRT SYSTEM   Photo courtesy of Boeing Aerospace Company

UTDC Light Rail Vehicle

The Urban Transportation Development Corporation, Ltd., (UTDC) of Toronto, Ontario, Canada, has produced a new light rail vehicle to be used on exclusive, semi-exclusive, or shared rights-of-way. The lower capital costs required for "light rail service" can allow construction of more transit route miles per dollar as compared with underground rapid transit. The vehicle can operate on streets or elevated platforms in a manner common to European cities.

In 1972, the city of Toronto decided to retain streetcar service in selected areas. The Toronto Transit Commission subsequently ordered 200 UTDC Light Rail Vehicles with deliveries scheduled for 1977.

The fully-loaded vehicle weighs 58,000 lbs (26,308 kg) and is scheduled to travel at 11 mph (18 km/hr). The use of solid-state controls with regenerative braking produces a 30% energy savings over conventional electric streetcars.

UTDC Advanced Technology Intermediate Capacity Transit System

A new system being developed by UTDC consists of small, quiet steel-wheeled trains for operation on street level, underground, or elevated rights-of-way. The lightweight trains will be about 120 feet (37 m) long and provide seating for 208 passengers. Propulsion and brakes will be executed by linear induction motors

UTDC LIGHT RAIL VEHICLE

Photo courtesy of
Urban Transportation
Development Corporation, Ltd.

mounted in the trucks. Disc and magnetic brakes will serve as emergency back-up.

An automated control system will allow for both driver and driverless operation of up to 20,000 passengers per hour.

UTDC ADVANCED TECHNOLOGY TRANSIT SYSTEM

Photo courtesy of Urban Transportation Development Corporation, Ltd.

Photo courtesy of Boeing Aerospace Company

Boeing PRT at the International Ocean Exposition, 1975

A system similar to the Boeing Morgantown PRT was used at the 1975 International Ocean Exposition in Okinawa, Japan. The system, produced by Boeing and Kobe Steel, Ltd., used sixteen computer-operated driverless cars over a 1.75 mile (2.8 km) stretch of two-way guideway. During the fair's six month run, the small rubber-tired electric cars carried four million riders.

Certain components of the system incorporated the StaRRcar concept originated by Alden Self-Transit Systems, Inc., of Natick, Maryland, U.S.A.

Ford "ACT"

The ACT, "Automatically Controlled Transportation," was developed by the Ford Motor Company for the public. Two ACT systems are implemented, one at the hotel Hyatt Regency, Dearborn, Michigan, and the other installed at Bradley International Airport near Hartford, Conn.

The system is quite literally a "horizontal elevator" which is electrically powered and computer controlled.

At the Hyatt Regency Dearborn installation, the bi-directional vehicles glide quietly on foam-filled tires over 2,600 feet (793 m) of elevated guideway between the Fairlane shopping complex and the hotel.

Each vehicle will cruise at 25 mph (40 km/hr), and will accommodate 24 passengers (10 seated, 14 standing). The two-car system can transport up to 1,800 people per hour.

Photo courtesy of Ford Motor Company

The "Electric Fireflies" of St. Louis

This neighborhood shuttle system, affectionately named "The Electric Fireflies," is run by FTM (Future Transportation Models) of St. Louis, Missouri, and operates in the Central West End area of the city.

The FTM is a non-profit corporation founded by Dr. Orville Brotherton, minister of one of the area's largest churches.

The trams, which are free to the rider, are supported by area merchants. The ten-passenger battery-powered chassis were supplied by Centron Systems. The trams are manufactured by Pargo, Inc., of Charlotte, N.C. New Exide lead-acid batteries produced by ESB, Inc., are being used as an on-road test by the battery manufacturer and double the range of each tram.

Photo courtesy of Union Electric, St. Louis, Missouri

ELECTROBUS   Photo courtesy of EVA-Chloride

The EVA-Chloride ElectroBus

The Electric Vehicle Associates, Inc. (EVA), and Chloride America, Inc., have formed EVA-Chloride ElectroBus, Inc., to produce and market the ElectroBus, a heavy-duty electric mass-transit vehicle.

Originally, the ElectroBus was developed by the Otis Elevator Company, which divested itself of on-road electric vehicle operation in 1976, selling all rights to EVA. Eleven ElectroBuses have been in transit operation for three years with an excellent performance record, including low operating and maintenance costs. The ElectroBus has been well received by the public.

A new ElectroBus development by EVA/Chloride ElectroBus, Inc., incorporates greater passenger capacity and efficiency. The ElectroBus is ideally suited for short haul, feeder, and shuttle operation. Power is supplied from a 156-volt traction battery through a thyristor (SCR) control, to a 65-kw heavy-duty traction motor. No transmission is used, because the motor is directly coupled to the differential. Acceleration is zero to 15 miles (24 km) per hour in six seconds and zero to 20 miles (32 km) per hour in ten seconds, with a full passenger load. The vehicle also uses regenerative braking, which reduces brake wear and returns recovered energy back to the batteries.

The 72-volt battery system averages 50 miles (80 km) at a cruising speed of 35 mph (56 km/hr) before recharging.

In 1978, the EVA/Chloride Corporation joint venture was dissolved, with all products merged into the Electric Vehicle Associates. The EVA now has sole responsibility for future ElectroBus plans.

Battronic Electric Bus

The Battronic Corporation of Boyertown, Pa., produces various electric buses. Two Battronic buses began serving a bus line in Montevideo, Minnesota, in June, 1978. Each 22-passenger vehicle operates over a 42 mile (67 km) route during a 6½ hour working day.

BATTRONIC ELECTRIC BUS

Photo courtesy of Lead Industries Association

SPECIALIZED ELECTRIC VEHICLES

Photo courtesy of E-Z-Go

E-Z-Go

The Polaris E-Z-Go Division of Textron, Inc., P.O. Box 388, Augusta, Georgia 30903, U.S.A., produces the E-Z Go. This is the latest generation of vehicles designed by a company which claims to be the largest producer of golf carts in the world. E-Z-Go golf carts have carried golfers over 400 million miles (644 million km) in the last two decades.

The basic E-Z-Go can be used as a golf cart, airport baggage or passenger carrier, and for maintenance, security, or a variety of industrial uses. Features include a weight of 960 lbs (436 kg) with batteries and a four-passenger capacity. Conversion kits can transform the basic E-Z-Go into a flatbed truck.

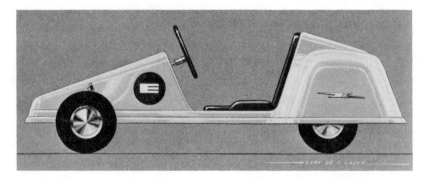

Eagle Electric Go-Cart

The Eagle is a one-passenger electric go-cart designed for children and adults for use on go-cart tracks or large paved areas and is not recommended for the street.

The vehicle features an all-welded racing frame with plastic molded body and contoured bucket seat. The 1 h.p. permanent magnet motor is powered through a 2-speed series-parallel contacter control from a 24-volt 70-ampere-hour battery system. Cruising time is 2 to 4 hours, with speeds of 8 to 15 mph (13 to 24 km/hr).

For more information write: Eagle Electric Go-Cart, 2237 Elliott Ave., Troy, Michigan 48084

BATRICADDY

BATRICAR
Photos courtesy Braune Batricar Ltd.

Braune Batricar

The Braune Batricar Limited of Stroud, England, manufactures a variety of small, electric-powered vehicles for utility, recreation, and handicapped persons.

The Batricar 4-wheeled electrically-driven invalid vehicle has a fiberglass body with pneumatic tires. The tiller steering control groups all controls together for one-hand driving. The infinitely-variable forward and reverse speed control system yields a top speed limit of 4 mph (6.4 km/hr) on level ground. The weight with one battery is 219 lbs (100 kg). The range is up to 6, 12, or 18 miles (9.6, 19, 29 km).

The new Batricar with bonnet has a top speed of 10 mph (16 km/hr). The Batricaddy is a golf cart designed to travel at 10 mph (16 km/hr) with a single seating capacity. A new version of the Batricaddy with a 40 mph (64 km/hr) maximum speed and 40 mile (64 km) range is due to be introduced presently. A 2 + 2 vehicle with the same performance will be introduced later.

Amigo

The Amigo is an electric vehicle designed for the elderly, handicapped, or for any application that would require a lightweight, highly maneuverable design. Powered by a 12-volt electric motor and battery, it is capable of continuous operation for three to four hours. The Amigo weighs 61 lbs (28 kg) less battery, and is available in four standard models including a mini-unit for children. It can be dismantled into four parts: seat, handle, battery, and base—for storage or transportation. The top speed is approximately 5 mph (8 km/hr) and is recommended for up to 150-lb (68 kg) riders. Heavier riders use a 3.5 mph (5.6-km/hr) version. The front-wheel-drive unit uses a 6-inch (150 mm) diameter front wheel.

For information write: Amigo Sales Inc., 6693 Dixie Highway, Bridgeport, Michigan 48722

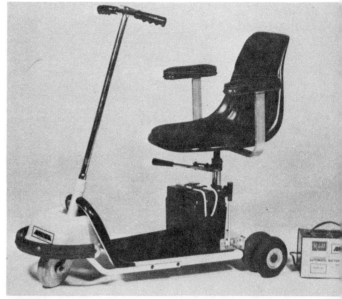

AMIGO

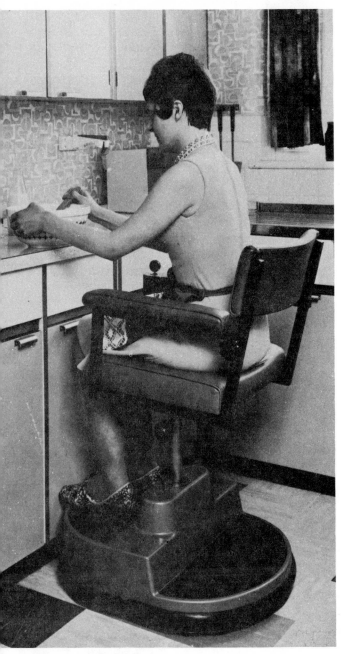

NEWTON QUEENSWAY

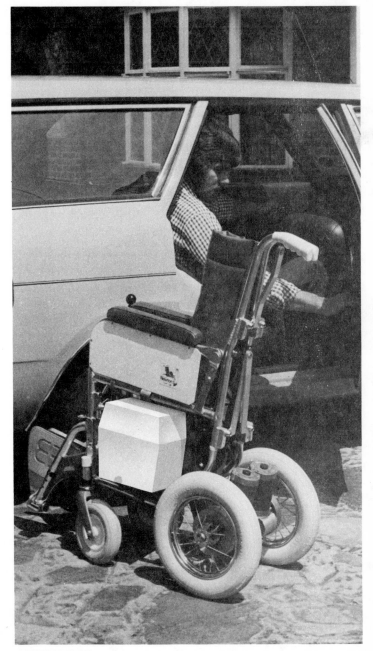

NEWTON ELAN

Newton Elan and Queensway

One important function of the electric vehicle is to provide freedom and mobility to the handicapped. Although the speeds of electric wheelchairs and handicap vehicles is usually very low, in the 1.9 mph to 3.8 mph (3 to 6.1 km/hr) range, the use of electric power in this application gives a true sense of independence to a great number of handicapped people throughout the world.

The Newton Elan is a folding electric wheelchair-type vehicle with a two-speed gearbox, two 12-volt batteries, fingertip control, independent suspension, with an aluminum frame. The Newton Queensway has both two speeds and two levels of height control and is quite literally a motorized swivel chair. Powered by two 6-volt batteries, the 87 lb (39 kg) vehicle has two speeds: .3 mph (.48 km) and .6 mph (.96 km). The range is approximately 2.5 miles (4 km). The weight is about 116 lbs (52 kg).

Electric-Powered Cycles

One of the simplest electric vehicle applications is the two- and three-wheeled cycle configuration.

The electric bicycle was patented in 1895, therefore the concept cannot be considered modern. Unfortunately, the early electric bicycles required heavy batteries and, consequently, heavy frames, wheels, and motors. Yet, some electric two-wheelers had highly ingenious designs, such as motors built into the wheel hub, thus eliminating belt or chain drive.

Modern application of battery and motor design now produces efficient, roadworthy, and economical products. Because of the moderate speeds and the lack of a cumbersome body, the electric bicycle can provide transportation at low cost and high kilowatt-per-hour efficiency.

The "fair weather" aspect of the electric bicycle complements the problems associated with poor battery performance during winter months. Electric bicycles are stored or unused during harsh weather, in the same manner as motorcycles.

And, finally, they are the least expensive of all electric vehicles. A low-cost electric kit which bolts onto a conventional bicycle is well within the budget of anyone. Senior citizens can attach a "helper" electric kit to their three-wheel trikes, and become free to shop and travel.

While there have been many electric-kit manufacturers in the last five years, the following companies have continued to produce and service their products. The companies mentioned can be contacted by those interested in electric kits. New kit manufacturers are occasionally advertised in the science magazines which are written for the general public.

Photo courtesy of Solo Motors, Inc., Newport News, Va.

Solo Electra

The German Solo Electra is a pedal-assisted electric scooter with a top speed of 16 mph (25 km/hr) and a maximum range of 25 miles (40 km) per charge. (Higher speeds are achieved with larger sprockets.) The Bosch 500-watt 24-volt permanent-magnet motor transfers power from two 12-volt, 40-ampere-hour batteries via a two-step vee belt and chain transmission with automatic centrifugal clutch. Front and rear drum brakes and shock absorbers are featured, with a tubular steel and epoxy plastic body.

The Solo Electra is distributed in the U.S. by the Odyssey Company, 112 Main Street, New Canaan, Conn. 06840, U.S.A.

Corbin Electric Motorcycle

The Corbin-Gentry Company of Somersville, Conn., U.S.A., has produced electric motorcycles since 1974.

The Corbin Electric motorcycle travels 30 to 40 miles (48 to 64 km) at 28-30 mph (45-48 km/hr) and weighs 386 lbs (174 kg) with batteries.

This vehicle uses a 1-hp series DC motor and is produced in a one- or two-speed version.

For more information write Corbin-Gentry, 40 Maple Street, Somersville, Conn., 06072, U.S.A.

Photo courtesy of Corbin-Gentry, Inc.

Photo courtesy of Transitron

Transitron I Motorcycle

The Transitron Company, formerly Charger Hawaii, has developed the Transitron I motorcycle as a test bed for new drive systems.

A new design-prototype automobile is now being finished which will include a "liquid battery recharging system" which allows for recharging in three minutes. The new Transitron electric car will not weigh more than five percent of a comparable piston-engined vehicle. The company claims that the vehicle will be a significant "breakthrough" upon completion.

The present Transitron I test motorcycle uses lead-acid batteries and weighs about 580 lbs (263 kg). A transistorized controller feeds power from 230 lbs (104 kg) of batteries to a separately excited motor. Top speed is 60 mph (97 km/hr). Range with conventional batteries is about 40 miles (64 km) per charge.

Information regarding vehicles should be directed to Transitron, Suite 412, 745 Fort Street, Hawaii Building, Honolulu, Hawaii 96815.

Eagle Picher 3-Wheel Motorcycle

The Eagle Picher Company of Joplin, Missouri, U.S.A., has produced this electric "trike" to demonstrate the energy density of their "silver-oxide-zinc" batteries, which have been used extensively in the U.S. space program in vehicles such as the "lunar rovers."

The vehicle carries less than 200 lbs (91 kg) of silver-oxide-zinc batteries and can travel 150 miles (241 km) at about 35 mph (56 km/hr). Two 1.5 hp permanent-magnet motors are used with a step-voltage-switching control.

The cost of silver batteries for a production vehicle is generally considered impractical; however, they are ideal for special non-transportation duties.

Photo courtesy of Eagle-Picher Company

General Engines Company

General Engines Company of New Jersey, U.S.A., has developed and marketed a line of electric mopeds and electric bicycle kits.

Their line of "Electropeds" also includes a three-wheeled trike for senior citizens or factory use.

For further information regarding the latest models and prices, contact General Engines Co., Electric Products Division, 591 Mantua Blvd., Sewell, N.J. 08080, U.S.A.

"Pedalpower" #50 Kit

The basic "Pedalpower" electric drive kit #50 uses a .5 hp permanent magnet motor with a friction drive that is designed to disengage for pedaling. The weight of the motor unit is 12 lbs (5.4 kg). Range for the model #50 is 25 miles (40 km) per charge. Another kit, the model #100, uses a 1 hp motor. A standard 12-volt light-utility battery supplies power.

"PEDALPOWER" #50 KIT Photo courtesy of General Engines Co. Inc., Electric Products Division

Electroped 6X2000

The Electroped 6X2000 utilizes a folding frame, which is ideal for campers. Features include a mono-shock, sealed-beam headlight, front-drum/rear-coaster brakes and a .5 hp friction-drive motor which yields a 25 mile (40 km) range. Total vehicle weight with battery is only 70 lbs (32 kg).

ELECTROPED 6X2000

Photo courtesy of General Engines Co. Inc., Electric Products Division

ELECTROSCOOTER

Photo courtesy of General Engines Co. Inc., Electric Products Division

"Electroscooter"

The "Electroscooter" features a 1.5 hp motor and variable belt transmission, which yields a top speed of 20 mph (32 km/hr) and range of 25 miles (40 km) per charge. Other features include front and rear drum brakes and telescopic shocks. Weight is 125 lbs (57 kg).

"Grocery Getter"

The "Grocery Getter" is a pedal trike with a 1 hp friction-drive motor. Range is 25 miles (40 km) per charge; speeds are 8-1/2 mph (19 km/hr) with no pedaling; 14 mph (23 km/hr) with motor and pedaling combined.

GROCERY GETTER

Photo courtesy of General Engines Co. Inc., Electric Products Division

Palmer Industries—Electric Cycle Kits

Palmer Industries of Endicott, New York, began developing electric drives long before the energy crisis of 1973-1974. The ''Electra Ride'' Kit, invented by Jack Palmer, features easy installation on over 100 various models of bicycles. Adaptation requires only an adjustable wrench and screwdriver and is accomplished without modifying the bicycle.

The 12-volt permanent-magnet, weatherproof motor is rated at 75% efficiency and disengages from the wheel to allow coasting. The friction-drive unit with clutch has only one moving part. A vinyl-coated steel battery case is designed to allow for battery maintenance without removal.

The Series-3 Kit features a 3/4-hp motor, a 17-mph (27-km/hr) speed and a 15-mile (24-km) range without pedal assist, using a light utility battery. The kit includes everything needed to convert a bicycle or adult tricycle to electric power, and carries a one-year warranty. Trike speed is 12 mph (19 km/hr).

PALMER ''ELECTRA RIDE'' SERIES 3 KIT

''Happy Wanderer''

The Palmer ''Happy Wanderer'' is an outdoor electric three-wheeler designed for handicapped or elderly use. Features include two forward and one reverse speed with single hand control. Range is 15 to 20 miles (24 to 32 km)

''HAPPY WANDERER''

EXECUTIVE MARK II

with speeds of 3 and 7 mph (5 and 11 km/hr). This vehicle is designed to operate on dirt or paved roads, wet or dry grass.

Executive Mark II Kit

The Executive Mark II model for bicycles and tricycles uses an industrial-rated 3/4-hp, ball-bearing, permanent-magnet motor with a two-year warranty.

Palmer Industries also makes a ''basic'' electric-drive kit using a 1/4-hp motor for those who wish only occasional use on flat terrain. In 1976, they also introduced an electric three-wheel industrial vehicle.

For more information and price list, contact Palmer Industries, P.O. Box 707, Endicott, N.Y. 13760, U.S.A.

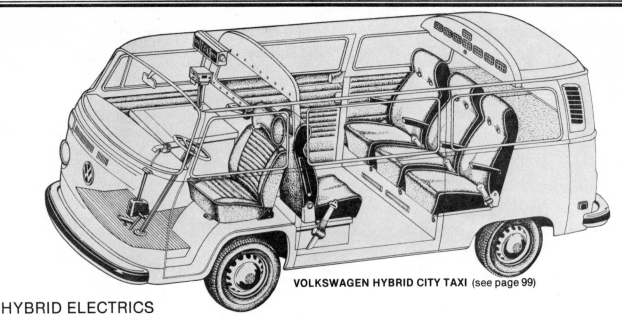

VOLKSWAGEN HYBRID CITY TAXI (see page 99)

HYBRID ELECTRICS

In the battery chapter, we mentioned "hybrid batteries," which combine more than one battery to produce a system which utilizes the strong points of each individual battery type.

The most commonly accepted hybrid electric vehicle is powered by an internal combustion or heat engine combined with a battery-electric system, such as the Volkswagen City Taxi described earlier.

In this combination, the electric motor provides additional power for rapid acceleration and other peak power demands while a comparatively small heat engine is used to enable the vehicle to cruise at higher speeds. The hybrid system is attractive because energy requirements at high speeds for a pure electric vehicle are quite high, while acceleration of a heat engine produces high pollution. In hybrid combination, these two systems can complement each other. The end result is lower pollution and a more efficient use of energy.

Another benefit is battery life. In a hybrid, there can be a higher battery cycle life because of the relatively shallow discharge cycles necessary to maintain operation of the vehicle.

All battery-hybrid-heat-engine vehicles are grouped into two classes: series and parallel. The series system takes the net power output of the heat engine and converts it into electricity through a generating system. The electric power is then converted to mechanical power via an electric motor connected to the drive wheels. The vehicle is then controlled as one would drive an ordinary electric vehicle. In this application the engine operates at a constant speed and load for maximum fuel economy. If the engine power output is greater than the vehicle's need at the time, the excess power is used to charge batteries. The use of regenerative braking can also capture kinetic energy otherwise lost.

In the parallel class of hybrids, power is delivered from the heat engine directly to the wheels through a transmission. Excess power is then used to charge the batteries. The electric motor in this type of system is driven by the heat engine to become a generator. When stopping the vehicle, the motor is used for regenerative braking. This type of system allows the use of gasoline power on the highway and all-electric power for city use. The parallel hybrid is more expensive to construct than the series, due to the mechanical transmission necessary for the gasoline or heat engine.

An application of the parallel system is to take a conventional automobile, fill the trunk with batteries, and attach an electric motor directly into the differential. The vehicle could then use a much smaller engine, perhaps a 4-cylinder instead of a V8. This system would give excellent acceleration due to the high torque provided by the electric motor from a standing start, and unlimited range due to the cruising capability of the heat engine.

An example of a series hybrid would be to attach a fuel-powered generator to an existing electric automobile, such as the Sebring Vanguard. The generating set would charge the battery pack while the vehicle was in use. At a standstill in traffic, the batteries would be charging while not in use.

The heat engine for a hybrid can be small. A

MERCEDES-BENZ HYBRID-ELECTRIC BUS (see page 98)

MAZDA TITAN HYBRID TRUCK (see page 101)

20-horsepower engine would be sufficient for a compact car while a 60-horsepower engine would be suitable for a van.

The diesel engine is highly efficient and has a high continuous power and long potential life. Perhaps it will be a candidate for hybrid vehicle use.

The rotary engine is another potential candidate for hybrids. It operates at a high rotational speed and can be coupled directly into a high-speed electric generator without a transmission. It is light, compact, and simple—and the durability of the rotary engine is at least as good as conventional piston engines because, with no valves, camshafts, and springs, there are fewer moving parts. In the United States, Europe, and Japan, new versions of rotary engines are being studied which are expected to have lower fuel consumption, lower emissions, and the ability to use a variety of fuels.

Another candidate is an external combustion type called the Stirling engine, which theoretically has high efficiency, low emissions, and is capable of using various fuels. The Ford Motor Company has fitted and test-driven vehicles with Stirling engines. United Stirling of Sweden has a series of five engines under development that vary in power output from 40 to 150 horsepower.

Gas-turbine engines are light, compact, durable and have low emissions. In aircraft use, gas turbine engines are highly developed; however, smaller versions, such as auxiliary power units, find their minimum fuel consumption too high for automotive applications. More work is being done in this area, and perhaps after additional research and development is accomplished, we will see a gas turbine in a hybrid vehicle.

Six types of hybrid urban buses have been built and several are in operation in Europe and Japan. As a result of successful operation, many hybrid buses are now on order for delivery during 1978-1980. These buses will be powered by both diesel and electric drive systems, using batteries, overhead trolley wires, or both. The hybrid concept for urban buses is appealing because of stop-and-go driving patterns, and because the space for batteries and drive system in a large bus is abundant.

Hybrids are generally regarded as unlimited-range vehicles because their range is determined by the size of their fuel tanks, which can be refilled. Unfortunately, range is limited when driven in the all-electric mode; however, the general concept of a hybrid is attractive, because most hybrids have been designed to have performance comparable to a conventional automobile. With the ability to accelerate, climb hills, and pass other vehicles at high speeds, hybrids break away from the generally accepted pattern of an electric vehicle. Some people feel that the electric hybrid is a stepping stone to pure electric vehicles. However, we must remember that hybrids are relatively expensive vehicles because of the components required to make them feasible. If the consumer price of a hybrid becomes astronomical, their market will be proportionately small. If hybrids can be made economically, they will be assimilated into the transportation market before all-electric automobiles, because of their speed and range advantage.

The Hybricon Centaur

The Centaur is a parallel hybrid prototype which operates on gasoline and/or electric power. While commuting at city speeds, up to 35 mph (56 km/hr), the Centaur runs on electric power using two G.E. motors, with electric clutches, connected to the rear wheels. Seven six-volt golf cart batteries, weighing 441 lbs (200 kg), provide about one hour of continuous driving in the "all-electric" mode.

The original vehicle was a Honda 600 sedan. The 32 hp aircooled internal combustion engine and front wheel drive have been retained to provide the components for gasoline powered operation.

For optimum economy, the vehicle starts out on electric power and shifts to gasoline power at about 30 mph (48 km/hr). This is an efficient use of the electric motors which operate more economically at low speed rather than high cruising speeds. Top speed under full gasoline power is 70 mph (113 km/hr).

During the gasoline driving mode, the motors are engaged, and act as generators to recharge the battery pack. One hour of driving at 50 mph (80 km/hr) under gasoline power will recharge the batteries up to 80% of a full charge. Additional driving will complete the recharging process, but at a slower rate. Combined range is 160 miles (257 km) per 4 gallons (15 liters) of gasoline.

The body of the 2,180 lb (990 kg) four passenger hybrid was styled by the famous automotive customizer, George Barris. The prototype vehicle was designed to attract a manufacturer who would produce the car in large quantities.

For more information, write: Hybricon, Inc., 11489 Chandler Boulevard, North Hollywood, California, 91601, USA.

The NRG Nitrogen-Electric Hybrid

The NRG Company of Peoria, Illinois, USA has designed a unique hybrid-electric truck. The electric motor is connected to a manual trans-

THE NRG NITROGEN-ELECTRIC HYBRID PICK-UP TRUCK.

mission, and a battery pack is located under the front hood. A tank in the rear holds cryogenically stored liquid nitrogen under low pressure.

The basic advantage of this series-type hybrid is the elimination of conventional overnight battery recharging. The batteries are continuously charged, as the vehicle is driven, by a small vane-type air turbine which is powered by the nitrogen as it expands, when changing from a cryogenic liquid into a gas.

The nitrogen lines are directed: from the tank, around the motor case and through pipes, (which also serve as the connecting cables for the batteries), and finally to a turbine pump motor. The turbine is connected, with a V-belt, to a 35 ampere alternator.

As the nitrogen expands from a liquid to a gas with the assistance of the heat generated by the motor and the battery cables, it turns the pump which runs the alternator that recharges the batteries. This patented system allows the flow of electricity to be almost resistance-free when travelling through super-cooled cables. In addition, the motor runs longer and more efficiently in a cooler mode. The batteries, operating under very shallow discharge cycles, will last longer then similar batteries which are constantly subjected to "deep discharging."

After the nitrogen passes through the air turbine, it can be directed to other pumps to do additional work, such as power steering and brakes. The cryogenic nitrogen is, of course, a natural air conditioning system. Through a heat exchanger, the nitrogen can also supply heat for the passenger compartment.

Nitrogen itself is an inert gas, totally non-flammable, non-volatile and non-toxic. Large volumes of nitrogen are now produced as a by-product of oxygen and argon manufacturing. Most of this nitrogen is unused and is returned to the atmosphere, although some is retained for commercial use such as cooling for cross-country food trucks. Currently, liquid nitrogen is about one fifth as expensive as gasoline in the U.S. The limitless source of nitrogen exists in two-thirds of the air we breathe. After it is expelled by the vehicle, it will return to the atmosphere, undiminished and unpolluted.

The range of a vehicle would be related to the amount of nitrogen carried and, of course, the weight of the vehicle and batteries. Conventional highway speeds could be maintained, and refilling the nitrogen tank, in a typical automobile, would take about as long as a gasoline fill-up, about every 500 miles.

The NRG Company claims that the Self-Charging System could be used to convert any conventional automobile, light truck, forklift or industrial application. Other uses would include boats, wheelchairs, emergency generators, and the conversion of conventional electric vehicles.

For more information, contact: Nitrogen NRG Company, 1230 W. Loucks Avenue, Peoria, Illinois, 61604, USA.

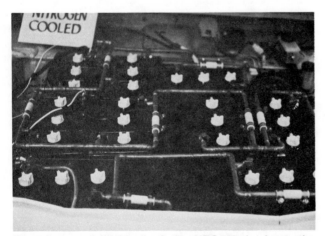

The nitrogen "plumbing" of the NRG truck shows the harness which carries the nitrogen through the battery compartment. The heat generated at the battery terminals helps liberate the nitrogen from a cryogenic liquid into a gas. When in use, the battery cables are covered with frost as the nitrogen cools the terminals allowing for reduced electrical resistance.

The NRG low-pressure liquid nitrogen tank is situated in the rear of the vehicle. In automotive use, a smaller tank could be stored in the trunk, taking up about as much space as a conventional gasoline tank. This tank can be filled at a truck stop in the same time as a gasoline powered vehicle. Nitrogen itself is inert and non-combustible insuring a high degree of safety in handling.

AN ELECTRIC VEHICLE USER SPEAKS OUT

Photos courtesy Gamma Photo Labs, Inc.

ELECTRIC DELIVERY BY GAMMA PHOTO LABS, INC.

Jerome August of Gamma Photo Labs in Chicago, Illinois, U.S.A., views the Sebring-Vanguard as the "Model-T of electric vehicles." He also feels a responsibility to "determine what's right—and what's wrong—with state-of-the-art electrics," and likens his experience with that of our great-grandfathers and their confrontation with early gas buggies. He feels that our grandfathers put up with a lot of problems which enabled us to have the comfortable and complex internal combustion vehicles of today—and we owe the same responsibility to our grandchildren so more efficient electrics will evolve.

In April, 1977, Mr. August purchased two Sebring-Vanguards for the purpose of daily film deliveries. The service area includes the Chicago Loop, one of the most congested and polluted metropolitan areas in the world. "On a normal 70 degree day, we get 25 and 30 miles per charge," Mr. August says. "Total mileage for both vehicles had reached the 5,000-mile mark by March, 1978. The top speed of 35 to 40 mph (56 km to 64 km/hr) is more than adequate for deliveries in the downtown Loop area."

Cold-weather operation did, however, propose some unique problems. On a winter day of about 20 degrees, the range was affected by the cold. "We remedied this situation by having one driver use both vehicles alternately during the day." Another problem was traction on slippery streets, due to the light vehicle weight and small tires. "But the light weight allows you to push it out of ruts easily." Yet another problem was winter cold. "We purchased a catalytic tent heater which helped keep the vehicle warm except on the coldest days below zero."

"The dependability rating is C+," he continued. "We had some problems with blown fuses—remedied by giving the driver the spare parts and a little bit of education on how to change them. You can't depend on gas stations for help; they look at the car with complete bewilderment and offer you a tow."

"Maintenance is simple; merely check battery water level every two weeks.

As far as economics, energy costs are about 1¢ per mile compared with 5-6¢ for a gasoline-powered vehicle."

There is one benefit Mr. August neglected to mention; that is the free advertising his company receives every time some Chicagoan says "Hey, that's an electric delivery car!"

SOME CONCLUSIONS

We have discussed a number of companies engaged in electric vehicle development. We have noticed that Ford, General Motors, Chrysler, and American Motors are studying and producing prototype battery-powered vehicles to prepare themselves for the coming of the electric vehicle.

It is evident, however, that large corporations which are sensitive to investors' needs are reluctant to invest the amount of money necessary to tool up for a production vehicle in a market that does not yet exist.

Perhaps the lead initiated by A. M. General Corporation, the subsidiary of American Motors that has produced the electric postal van, will be followed by other large companies. Besides accumulating data from real life, A. M. General is also in a position to mass-produce postal vehicles when necessary.

If you recall from the history chapter, we noted that no electric vehicles were ever mass-produced. Some people have maintained that mass production would have reduced the cost of early electric vehicles in the way that the Model T responded to efficient production techniques. To date, the Sebring-Vanguard has been the only relatively mass-produced electric passenger car. Its production volume is about 2,000 vehicles. With the potential of the German GES Combine entry into the electric vehicles market, their Volkswagen-manufactured van may be the first real mass-produced electric vehicle ever made.

If the new generation of electric automobiles is not reliable and absolutely flawless, its chances of success in today's economy will be poor. The only way to achieve this is to allow the exacting scientific tests and solid engineering necessary before any product is offered to the public.

Controllers and battery hardware must be developed to their full technological potential so their operation will be absolutely reliable. This approach will help the public to accept electric vehicles and will encourage positive word-of-mouth publicity from those who own them.

There is no force as destructive as bad publicity in any industry. We have seen products disappear almost overnight from the marketplace when the public is either frightened because of a safety or health hazard or, even worse, indifferent.

A recent U.S. Government publication has deemed today's electric vehicle industry "immature." Tests of various state-of-the-art vehicles proved less than satisfactory in terms of overall performance. Maintenance records exhibited many problems associated with most on-road vehicles. In truth, the electric vehicle industry is not immature; it is embryonic. But this tiny embryo will grow, because the stage is set for one of the most meteoric rises ever witnessed by the financial community.

Photo shows a clay model, under intensive study by General Motors design engineers who feel that battery-powered vehicles have a distinct place in the future of transportation. The clay model is a further step along the design path as technicians move closer to what could be the shape of an electric car of the future.

Photo courtesy General Motors Corporation

Home-Built Electric Vehicles

While the sophisticated laboratories of vehicle manufacturers in Japan, Germany, France, England, and the United States are developing prototype, test-bed, and pie-in-the-sky vehicles, the largest group of on-road electrics are developed in the basements and garages of thousands of do-it-yourself vehicle builders.

Many electric vehicle clubs and organizations have been formed to assist would-be inventors and fabricators. No one exactly knows when the phenomena began, but I suppose there were people installing motors into carriages and buckboards before Henry Ford's time. The notion of putting together a vehicle from scratch, or converting one thing into something else, can result in some extremely roadworthy vehicles.

As with many other hobbies, once a person is bitten by the bug, all financial rationale can go out the window. The pride in building something that is both practical and relatively exotic becomes the motivating force behind the majority of these projects. There is no feeling in the world like the one you get when a person comes up to you and says, ''You mean you really built that yourself?''

Thomas Edison left a small seed of inspiration to all who have longed to build, design, and invent without worrying about large corporations dictating marketing strategies or pulling the strings. When you build your own electric, you can say to yourself, "Hey, I'm as good as General Motors, Ford, or Chrysler. I've put a working vehicle on the road."

As you will see in some of these examples in this chapter, the spirit of the home builder, inventor, and entrepreneur is certainly not dead in this country. In fact, it isn't even anywhere near dying. The clubs listed in this chapter may be contacted for further information.

PLEASE NOTE: Any build-it-yourself kits mentioned are sold directly through the kit manufacturers and have no relationship with the author or the publisher of this book.

Therefore, as with any purchase, the buyer must be aware of the potential problems that may arise. You would not attempt, for example, to build a complete electric car with fiberglass body if you did not have the knowledge of tools necessary to build a bookcase. Beginning any project such as this, one must understand the costs and possibility of undisclosed expenses. Remember, that after tallying up the prices for batteries, motors, controllers, frames, switches, wiring, and all the unseen expenses such as possible machining, welding, and fabricating, you may not be able to afford to build your own vehicle. In this case, it would, in my opinion, be unwise to start.

However, to those of you who do have the basic knowledge of tools and are familiar with other build-it-yourself projects, and are willing to tackle something as large as building an automobile, I can think of no better project to which you can dedicate your time. Sure, you can build a helicopter, plane, or boat. But none

of these have the ability to provoke public interest, awe, and envy as does driving your own electric vehicle down a main street on a summer day.

It would be impossible to describe all of the home-built electric vehicles in the United States, because of their vast numbers. Therefore, I have selected a few that are typical of this avocation.

Stockberger—Pinto

John Stockberger, a data specialist supervisor in Chicago, Illinois, has converted a 1971 Ford Pinto to electric power. The 2900 lb (1315 kg), 4-passenger automobile weighs only 500 lbs (227 kg) more than a standard Pinto.

Stockberger purchased a surplus U.S. aircraft generator through an advertisement in *Popular Mechanics* magazine for $100.

The motor was originally manufactured during World War II by the Jack & Heintz Company, and would cost over $1500 if produced today.

The Pinto had a burned-out engine when Stockberger found it in a wrecking yard. Its initial cost was $200. Therefore, the vehicle, complete with sixteen golf-cart batteries reflected an investment of $1200 total—plus a tremendous amount of spare-time work.

The batteries are carried in the trunk and partially up front with the motor. A standard transmission and clutch arrangement is used yielding 25 mph (40 km/hr) in first gear and 40 mph (64 km/hr) in second gear. (Third and fourth gears and the clutch are not used.)

Speed control is accomplished through voltage switching in four steps from 12 to 48 volts. The car is capable of speeds in excess of 40 mph (64 km/hr) and acceleration from zero to

STOCKBERGER PINTO

BATTERIES AND MOTOR OF STOCKBERGER PINTO

30 mph (48 km/hr) in 15 seconds. The approximate maximum range is about 40 miles (64 km) per charge, although no test for exact range has been made. Recharging is achieved with an on- board charger using a standard 15-amp, 120-volt electrical outlet.

The automobile was completed in the winter of 1974. Since the summer of 1975, it has been in daily service commuting between the train station and John Stockberger's home in Batavia, Illinois—a round trip of 16 miles (26 km). Cost of operation, including electricity and bat-

tery replacement, is about 5 cents per mile (3¢ per km). Distilled water for the batteries is obtained by capturing the dehumidifier by-products from his home furnace/air conditioner.

Mr. Stockberger is the president of the Fox Valley Electric Auto Association, Rt. 1, Box 549, Batavia, Illinois 60510, U.S.A.

William H. Shafer—DAF

In 1976, Bill Shafer, an engineer for Commonwealth Edison Company in Chicago, Illinois, converted a Dutch automobile, the DAF, to electric drive. Since then he has traveled 2218 miles (3570 km) and consumed 1108 kwh of electrical energy, or 0.5 kwh per mile (0.31 kwh per kilometer).

The vehicle carries four golf-cart batteries positioned over the rear axle and two golf-cart plus two SLI batteries in front.

A pump located in the rear trunk activates the Variomatic, continuously-variable ratio transmission. Speed is controlled by voltage switching 12, 24, and 36 volts to the motor armature. Top speed of the vehicle is 35 mph (56 km/hr); range is 21 miles (34 km); weight is 1800 lbs (816 kg), of which about 500 lbs (227 kg) is batteries.

Bill Shafer is a member of the Fox Valley Electric Auto Association of Illinois.

WILLIAM H. SHAFER AND THE ELECTRIC DAF

Ken Myers—NSU

Ken Myers, another member of the Fox Valley Electric Auto Association, has converted a 1971 NSU 1200 to electric power. This vehicle carries only enough batteries to travel a 12-mile daily trip to work and back.

Eight six-volt golf-cart batteries power a 28-volt, 200-amp surplus shunt wound aircraft DC generator. Speed control is through battery switching in eight 6-volt steps and the transmission. First gear yields 21 mph (34 km/hr), and 42 mph (68 km/hr) is obtained in second gear. (Third and fourth gears are not used.)

One 12-volt accessory battery provides field current to the motor and power for accessories. The car weighs 1965 lbs (891 kg) which is only 100 lbs (45 kg) more than the conventional vehicle.

NSU CONVERTED BY KEN MYERS

ELECTRIC POWERED
VOLKSWAGEN CON-
VERTED BY ROY
KAYLOR, JR.

Roy Kaylor, Jr.—VW

Roy Kaylor, Jr., a Menlo Park, California, engineer, has built a prototype fiberglass-bodied Volkswagen conversion.

This sleek sportscar has a curb weight of 1850 lbs (839 kg). Range is 70 miles (112 km) at 50 mph (80 km/hr). Under optimum conditions, the vehicle can travel 120 miles (193 km) at about 35 mph (56 km/hr). In 1976, a freeway test over a 7200-foot (2200 m) pass yielded a 90-mile (145 km) range from Nevada to California.

A 30-hp compound wound motor, with up to a 100-hp peak, is powered through a fully transistorized controller by a 72-volt, 220-amp-hour battery set. The conventional VW transmission and clutch are retained to allow even greater speed flexibility.

Mr. Kaylor is a member of the Electric Auto Association, a California-based club.

Kits of this and other VW conversion models are available through Kaylor Energy Products, 1927 Menalto Ave., Menlo Park, California 94025, U.S.A.

Paul Brasch—VW

Another Volkswagen conversion is this fiberglass sports car built by Paul Brasch of San Jose, California.

Power from the fourteen 12-volt batteries is supplied to a rewound Jack & Heintz motor. Top speed is 70 mph (112 km/hr).

Mr. Brasch is a member of the Electric Auto Association of California.

ELECTRIC POWERED
VOLKSWAGEN CON-
VERTED BY PAUL
BRASCH

**VOLKSWAGEN CON-
VERTED BY JOHN
NEWELL**

John Newell—VW

John Newell of Belmont, California, has constructed a fiberglass sportcar based on a VW chassis.

The most distinctive feature about this vehicle is that it carries 600 lbs (272 kg) of nickel-cadmium batteries. Power is applied to a Jack & Heintz 9-1/2-hp aircraft motor by battery- switching controls. The curb weight of the vehicle is 2,000 lbs (907 kg).

Mr. Newell is the president of the Electric Auto Association of California. The EAA currently mails over 500 copies of its newsletter throughout the U.S., Canada, Mexico, Australia, South America, and South Africa.

The EAA is a non-profit organization formed in 1967 by Walter Laski, now the editor of the newsletter. For a sample of the newsletter, mail a self-addressed, stamped envelope to Walter V. Laski, 1674 Merrill Drive, Apt. 12, San Jose, California 95124, U.S.A.

In California, the EAA has chapters in the following cities: San Francisco, Bakersfield, Contra Costa, East Bay, Marin, Santa Clara and Peninsula.

For EAA membership information, send a self-addressed, stamped envelope to Mr. John Newell, 1249 Lane St., Belmont, California 94022, U.S.A.

A list of electric vehicles owned or built by EAA members:

TYPE	NUMBER
N.S.U. Prinz	5
Panhard Corvair	1
V.W. Bug	4
Opel	1
Renault Caravelle	3
Custom Built plywood body	1
Motorcycle	6
V.W. Dune Buggy	2
Pinto	1
V.W. Fiberglass body	2
Toyota	1
V.W.	11
Renault La Dauphine	3
Ottis	1
Lloyd	1
Subaru	1
Model "T" Ford	2
M.G.	2
3 wheel Aurenthetic	1
Bicycle	2
Renault Gordini	1
SAAB Station Wagon	1
Corvair	1
Fiat	2
Austin American	1
Sunbeam Imp.	1
Custom-built 1904 Olds	1
Custom dragster	1
GoGo Mobile	1
CitiCar	1
Kharman Ghia	11
Renault special customs	5
Custom designed & others	23
Total number of EAA vehicles	101

LEOPOLD SCHATZL AND HIS 1960 ELECTRO-PRINZ

SIMCA EV CONVERTED BY LEO SCHATZL

STERLING EV CONVERTED BY LEO SCHATZL

Leopold Schatzl

Leopold Schatzl drove his electrically-converted NSU Prinz over 8,000 miles (12,875 km) between early 1973 to mid-1975. This was the first electric vehicle produced by the Ontario, California, electronics technician.

The Electro-Prinz is a 1960 NSU German subcompact which only weighed 1,200 lbs (545 kg) in its original form. The conversion was made possible with a surplus 10-hp aircraft starter-generator. Speeds of 25 mph (40 km/hr) and 40 mph (64 km/hr) with a range of 40 miles (64 km) per charge are achieved with the 36-volt, 220-amp-hour battery pack. The original six 175-amp-hour golf-cart batteries were exchanged for six 220-amp-hour units in 1975.

In 1975, Mr. Schatzl converted a 1965 Simca 1000, and presently is completing a Sterling, fiberglass-bodied sportscar.

Richard Ness—Electric Bicycle

Richard Ness is a Chicago, Illinois, machinist who has built two electric bicycles.

His first model, the ''land-ark'', uses a one-horsepower DC traction motor and belt drive to the rear wheel. A reinforced frame and rear wheel help carry the two 12-volt SLI batteries, rated at 80-amp-hours each.

The vehicle has two forward speeds, 15 mph (24 km/hr) and 30 mph (48 km/hr). Range at 15 mph (24 km/hr) is 30 miles (48 km) and 15 miles (24 km) at 30 mph (48 km/hr). This electric bike has been in service for three years.

Mr. Ness recently completed building a lighter weight electric bike with belt drive and a higher speed motor.

TWO BICYCLES BUILT BY RICHARD NESS

Sheldon Shacket—Electric Touring Bike

Sheldon Shacket, the author of this book, has built over 15 two and three-wheeled electric vehicle prototypes.

The Model Three is a lightweight electric bicycle built on a Raleigh three-speed frame. Power from the type 27 marine battery, rated at 95 amp hours, is directed through a single-speed on/off switch. The motor is a 1/2 hp,

permanent-magnet type with vee-belt drive to the rear wheel. Range is 20 miles (32 km) at 16 mph (26 km). Top speed is 18 mph (29 km).

Other vehicles built include a 2-wheeled vehicle with a top speed of over 50 mph (81 km) and another long-range bicycle with a 35 to 50 mile (56-81 km) range at 16 mph (26 km) using 2 golf-cart batteries.

ELECTRIC TOURING BIKE BUILT BY SHELDON SHACKET

VOLKSWAGEN EV CONVERTED WITH CORBIN-GENTRY KIT

Corbin-Gentry Electric Bug Kit

The Corbin-Gentry Company produces a conversion called the ''Electric Bug Kit'' which is designed to convert a standard Volkswagen to electric power. The kit consists of everything needed for the conversion including a DC motor, adaptor plate, contactor assembly and battery charger. Batteries are not included.

A converted V.W. can travel 40 to 50 miles (64 to 80 km) at 40 to 50 mph (64 to 80 km/hr) using twelve batteries. Higher speeds can be achieved by increasing battery voltage to the motor.

For more information contact: Corbin-Gentry, Inc., 40 Maple Street, Somersville, Connecticut 06072, U.S.A.

KING CONVERSION SPORTS MODEL

EV CONVERSION KIT PRODUCED BY KING ENGINEERING

King Conversion Kits

King Engineering of Clay, New York, produces electric conversion kits for Volkswagen Bugs, squarebacks, fastbacks, and vans. The basic kit includes all components necessary for the conversion except batteries. A DC motor is connected directly to the VW transaxle. The kit includes cables, controller with regenerative braking, battery charger, and motor cooling fan. The vehicle shown is a King Conversion which won honors at the Third Annual Mt. Washington Alternative Vehicle Regatta. The car successfully climbed Mt. Washington with three passengers aboard.

The sports model has a top speed of 55 mph (88 km/hr), and a range of 60 to 70 miles (97 to 113 km) at a constant 40 mph (64 km/hr).

For more information regarding the conversion kit prices, contact: King Engineering, 5436 Topsfield Lane, Clay, New York 13041 U.S.A.

ELECTRIC CAR CLUBS

For membership information please contact the following Electric Automobile Club in your area:

Electric Auto Association (EAA)
1674 Merrill Drive No. 12
San Jose, CA 95124
Central Office—(408) 264-8936

EAA Chapters: Santa Clara, Peninsula, San Francisco, Sacramento, Northbay, Contra Costa, Eastbay, Bakersfield.

Fox Valley EAA
Rt. 1 Box 549
Batavia, IL 60510

Denver EV Council
Rt 3 Box 700
Golden, CO 80401

EV Assn. of Ohio
445 Basset Road
Bay Village, OH 44140

Electric Vehicle Society
1114 Superba St.
Venice, CA 90291

Electric Vehicle Ass'n.
P.O. Box 1840
Fontana, CA 92335

Electric Vehicle Ass'n.
34 Berkeley Square
London W1X 6AJ
England

Australian EV Ass'n.
95 Collins Street
Melbourne 3000
Australia

Contemporary Legislation

We have discussed the participation of the German and Japanese governments regarding legislative impetus applied to electric vehicle development. Other activity is underway in Sweden, France, Italy, England, USSR, The Republic of China, and Taiwan. In each case, government and business efforts are tied together for mutual achievement.

The United States has one ongoing government program which was passed into law on September 17, 1976, after a Congressional override of a presidential veto. Public Law 94-413 is The Electric and Hybrid Vehicle Research and Demonstration Act of 1976. The Act is designed to promote electric and hybrid vehicle research and development and to provide up to 7,500 demonstration vehicles within 72 months of the enactment of the law.

The entire program is under the jurisdiction of the Energy Research and Development Administration (ERDA), now a part of the Department of Energy (DOE).

Presently, the electric auto industry in the U.S. is a composite of equipment and component manufacturers. These entrepreneurs assemble electric cars in small numbers. The largest manufacturer to date is the Sebring

Vanguard company which has produced a total of only 2,000 cars in the last few years.

Public Law 94-413 is designed to stimulate small businesses to develop electric vehicle technology.

The first phase of the Act called for a study of current "state-of-the-art" electric vehicles. The next stage will define performance standards and contract the purchase of 2,500 demonstration vehicles. The final phase calls for the delivery of 5,000 demonstration vehicles with higher performance standards. On February 25, 1978, several amendments to the E/HV Act of 1976 were signed into law by President Carter after passing both houses of Congress. One provision of the amendments allows purchasers of electric vehicles a tax credit equal to 10% of the vehicle's price. Other provisions of the Amendments allow for an extended period of demonstrations through 1986, and for the acquisition of a total of 10,000 vehicles, compared with the 7,500 indicated in the original Public Law 94-413.

Other provisions for near-term electric vehicle demonstrations call for four small manufacturers to produce two vehicles each. This contract awards each manufacturer $100,000 to cover the cost of both vehicles.

The U.S. government goal is to reduce oil imports and increase employment by helping industry develop an integrated electric vehicle market. Prospects of replacing a good proportion of the U.S. "second" and "third" cars with electric vehicles could account for up to 26-million electric automobiles by the year 2000. This is a potential savings of about 400 million barrels of oil per year.

The infusion of government money, up to $160 million in a seven year period, will stimulate industry to develop the subsystems and the infrastructure necessary to allow the electric automobile and truck to be mass produced in the United States.

General Electric/Department of Energy Demonstration Vehicle

The U.S. Department of Energy has awarded a $6 million two-year contract to the Research and Development Center of General Electric Company in Schenectady, New York, for development and construction of two 4-passenger experimental electric automobiles. The subcompact electrics are powered by lead-acid battery systems and based on a design developed jointly by General Electric and Chrysler Corporation. These "integrated test vehicles" are designed for an urban driving cycle of 75 miles (121 km) per charge with a top speed of 55 mph (89 km/hr) and special attention given to stop-and-go driving. Each vehicle carries 18 Globe-Union batteries and incorporates regenerative braking.

The DOE has instructed the developers to design the electrics with special consideration given to mass production techniques to enable the purchase price and operating costs to compare with conventional automobiles. The two electrics were designated for a spring, 1979 delivery to the Department of Energy. The illustrations shown are a guide to the projected vehicle design. Consideration has been made for ease of battery maintenance and passenger comfort. (See page 143)

Garrett DOE Vehicle

The Garrett AiResearch Company of California

DOE/GE/CHRYSLER ELECTRIC CAR

Photo courtesy of General Electric Company

has been awarded a $5 million dollar contract by the U.S. Department of Energy (DOE) to build two electric demonstration vehicles.

Under the DOE Near Term Electric Vehicle Program, Phase II, the two vehicles were scheduled for delivery in April, 1979.

The proposed vehicle design features a regenerative flywheel/electric motor configuration which has a projected range of 94 miles (151 km), a cruising speed of 55 mph (89 km/hr) and a 70-mph (112 km/hr) passing speed.

The low-profile four-passenger automobile weighs 2,566 lbs (1163 kg) including 1,040 lbs (471 kg) of lead-acid batteries. The controller is a solid-state, digital micro-processor which will also monitor the use of regenerative braking and flywheel demand. The motor and generator are both separately excited DC units which are developed specifically for electric commuter car duty.

One outstanding feature of the design is the use of a high-speed flywheel which can store kinetic energy to be used for acceleration and passing. By reducing the proper battery discharge rate during acceleration, the flywheel will insure long battery life and maximize the total available energy. The flywheel is a fiber glass-wound cylindrical rotor with a tapered-spoke aluminum hub, housed in a low-pressure aluminum chamber. The key to the system lies in the ability of the microprocessor to distinguish the needs of the motor, generator, flywheel, and battery.

The Garrett Company has extensive flywheel experience and is one of the Signal Companies, which employs over 13,000 people. Subcontractors for this project include The Brubaker Group for body design and All American Racers for suspension design.

DOE/GE/TRIAD Electric Vehicle

An experimental vehicle design was funded by the DOE under a $265,000 contract in 1976. The co-developers are the General Electric Company, Chrysler Corporation, Triad Services, Inc. (a design firm), and ESB, Inc.

The DOE contract calls for an experimental short trip vehicle with a 55 mph (88 km/hr) top speed and acceleration of 0 to 30 mph (48 km/hr) in ten seconds. Range for stop and go cycle is 75 miles (120 km) per charge. Other goals are: A $5,000 (1975 U.S. Dollars) mass produced price, with a minimum life of 100,000 miles (160,000 km).

The vehicle is designed to use advanced lead-acid batteries, regenerative braking, and microprocessor electronic controls. The 2,942 lb (1350 kg) vehicle will carry 1182 lbs (536 kg) of batteries.

DOE/GARRETT AiResearch CAR

Photo courtesy of Garrett AiResearch

DOE/GARRETT AiResearch CAR

Photo courtesy of Garrett AiResearch

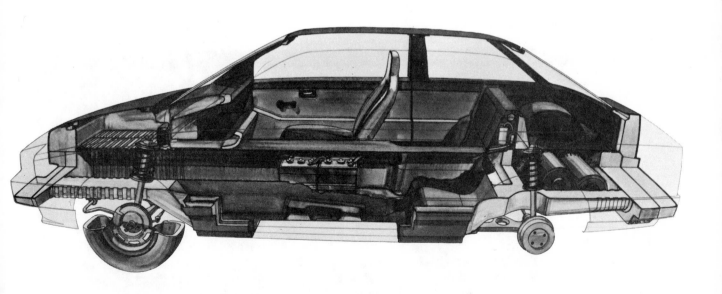

DOE/GE/TRIAD

Photo courtesy of General Electric Company

G.E. DELTA

An earlier experimental electric was designed by GE to test components such as batteries, motors and controllers.

The DELTA (Developmental Electric Town Car) weighs 2400 lbs (1088 kg) which includes 920 lbs (417 kg) of batteries. Top speed is 55 mph (88 km/hr) and acceleration is zero to 25 mph (40 km/hr) in six seconds. The DELTA uses a hybrid battery system composed of a lead-acid main battery and a nickel-cadmium booster battery. Range is up to 120 miles (193 km) on level terrain at about 35 mph (56 km/hr). A special DC motor with solid state controls and front wheel transaxle drive are also featured.

Gould Electric Van

Two electric vans are being produced by Gould Inc., with the prospect of constructing up to 500 additional vans in 1979. One van is designed for service and delivery duty, the other is directed toward personal use with a 12 passenger capacity.

The vehicles are designed to meet or exceed the DOE performance standards for state-of-the-art electric vehicle technology. For commercial vehicles, these requirements are as follows: the vehicle must accelerate from 0 to 31 mph (50 km/hr) in 15 seconds, and be able to maintain a speed of 46.5 mph (75 km/hr) for 5 minutes. Range can be no less than 31 miles

Photo courtesy of General Electric Company

G.E. DELTA

GOULD ELECTRIC VAN

Bob McKee, left, and John McClung discuss plans for the Gould electric vans. In the background is a working drawing of the completed van design.

(50 km) per charge. An 80% deep discharged battery must be recharged in no more than 10 hours. After twelve months of 9,400 miles (15,100 km), the battery system must be capable of 75% of the vehicles range and meet minimum performance levels.

Both of the Gould vehicles are Ford E250 Vans which have been converted by Gould and McKee Engineering. Each van carries 2,200 lbs. (998 kg) of Gould advanced lead-acid batteries with a new grid design which yields 50% longer battery life. Overall motor efficiency has been improved thereby reducing power losses by 50% compared with previous Gould systems.

Gould Inc. is interested in building vans for the DOE electric vehicle demonstrations. Under Phase I of the program, 200 to 400 electric vehicles are scheduled to be purchased by site operators. These operators can then sell or lease vehicles to business or private users.

The Gould Company is well known for its line of batteries. Presently the company is researching advanced lead-acid batteries and new high energy density nickel-zinc batteries with controlled field tests scheduled for 1979.

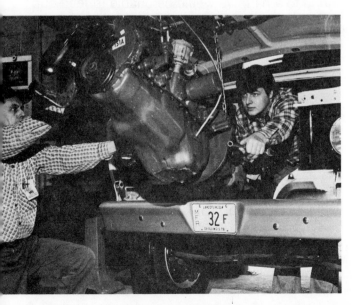

Mechanics at McKee Engineering, Inc. remove the internal combustion engine from one of the vans being converted. The entire nose of the vehicle is rebuilt out of fiberglass in order to reduce weight and aerodynamic drag.

Meeting Our Future Energy Needs

HOW WE WILL MEET OUR FUTURE ENERGY NEEDS

If we are to have electric vehicles in the future, we must have the capacity to generate electric power. Power to run our cities, power for our farms, our cars and airplanes. Without energy, our cities would freeze, transportation would grind to a halt, we would be unable to feed our people—our world would be virtually uninhabitable. The power must come from somewhere, and it must be plentiful. Where will this power come from?

We can no longer depend upon our free fossil-fuel reserves. Free, because we do not pay for their production or replacement costs. Since you cannot produce oil, you are merely charged for the privilege of pumping it out of the ground. Oil is nature's gift. Some day the free ride will be over. Today, power-generating stations cannot supply electric home heating that can compete with oil heat. Oil is so artificially inexpensive, we can't afford to use anything else economically. In the future, when we will be crying out for oil to use for lubrication, personal transportation, aircraft, and the specialized applications for which oil has no substitute, we will wish that today's oil had been more expensive.

Only the cost of extraction and refining, not the "dearness" value is included in the market price of today's oil. In these terms oil is practically free. We don't produce oil; it is the result of a multi-million-year process. You won't find it on the moon or any other planet because it is a product of life.

Therefore, we need to seek out more plentiful sources which will provide us with unlimited power. We must then connect the power to our homes, factories, vehicles, and cities. One solution is to establish a society whose energy is based on electricity and hydrogen. There is a possibility that together, they can provide for all of our needs.

New methods for electricity production will be developed and old methods refined. Hydrogen can help supplement natural gas and other fossil-fuels. Hydrogen can also be used to "store" energy, to increase power plant efficiencies. The concept of an economy based on hydrogen is one outlook for the future.

The idea of a totally electric "hydrogen economy" is not new; its potential application to our society has been extolled by some scientists for many years. It may or may not make sense to you, but it does offer a method to acquire the electric power necessary to achieve the goals of future transportation.

HYDROGEN

In "The Mysterious Island" written by Jules Verne in 1874, a reference was made to hydrogen power. One character responded to a question about what would happen if we ran out of coal and other fuels. He said, "Yes, my friends, I believe that water will one day be employed as fuel, that hydrogen and oxygen which constitute it, used singly or together, will furnish an inexhaustible source of heat and light . . ."

The sources of energy with hydrogen as a backbone could lead to the construction of a worldwide network of inexhaustible, clean power that will be both compatible with nature and with the desire for man to rise above his present state of development.

Hydrogen may be an alternative to natural gas. If natural gas is the first fossil fuel source to be depleted, hydrogen could be used as a substitute in our pipelines. Perhaps at first the hydrogen will be mixed with natural gas products, and then with synthetic gas derived from coal gasification.

Compared with natural gas, hydrogen cannot produce the heat value volume for volume, and the cost of hydrogen is far greater than natural gas. However, the impetus of higher gas prices could eventually close the price gap.

How powerful is hydrogen as a fuel? Liquid hydrogen has been powering rocket vehicles from the very beginning of our space program. The first practical hydrogen and oxygen fuel cells were used to supply electric power to virtually all U.S. spacecraft. So we can see that hydrogen is a valuable power source.

Hydrogen-powered automobiles have been built. After studying their advantages, perhaps solutions to storage and safety problems will make hydrogen transportation an integral part of a 21st Century society.

Vehicle demonstrations have shown that hydrogen: (1) burns more efficiently in a lean air mixture than does gasoline, (2) burns cooler than gasoline with a non-luminous flame, (3) allows the use of ultra-high compression ratios, thereby increasing the horsepower of the engine, and (4) is virtually non-polluting.

Because any heat engine can basically be converted to use hydrogen, some scientists see the hydrogen-oxygen engine as the successor to the fossil fuel internal-combustion engine.

Hydrogen was proposed as a fuel for engines in the early 1800's. (Hydrogen itself was discovered in 1766 by Cavendish.) Efforts were made in 1923 by the British engineer, Sir Harry Ricardo, to convert an internal-combustion engine to hydrogen.

There are three basic combinations that use hydrogen for fuel in an internal combustion engine: hydrogen-air, hydrogen-gasoline, and hydrogen-oxygen. A number of hydrogen-air vehicles were entered by several universities as student projects in the Urban Vehicle Design Competition of 1972. Later a group of U.C.L.A. engineering students continued to work on their hydrogen-converted 1972 Gremlin, using a specially-modified Ford V8 engine. The hydrogen was stored as a gas in two commercial cylinders mounted behind the front seats. The two cylinders weighed 300 pounds (136 kg) each, carried six pounds (2.7 kg) of hydrogen stored at 6,000 psi (422 kg/cm²), allowing for a total range of about 60 miles (96 km). A top speed of over 90 mph (145 km/hr) was recorded.

One driving report indicated that smooth and detonation-free acceleration could be achieved when the vehicle was full-throttled at ten mph (16 km/hr) in high gear. In an emission test conducted in 1973, the U.C.L.A. Gremlin registered zero hydrocarbon and carbon monoxide emissions. Later, students at Brigham Young University employed water injection techniques to lower combustion temperatures and increase power.

Another U.C.L.A. experiment used a four-cylinder Datsun engine designed to burn liquid hydrogen, stored at −423°F (−253C), which is only 37° (21C) above absolute zero. Special cryogenic storage tanks with a capacity of 50 gallons, were used. Each thermos-bottle type container weighed 50 pounds (23 kg) and carried 30 pounds (14 kg) of fuel which gave the Datsun pickup a range of 600 miles (965 km).

A more recent U.C.L.A. project included a design for a hydrogen-powered U.S. Postal Service delivery truck which carried liquid hydrogen in a cryogenic storage tank with water injection to reduce emissions and backfiring. A regular gasoline tank was used to store the water required. The range for the vehicle was 450 miles (724 km) at normal driving speeds, consuming 30 pounds (14 kg) of hydrogen. Since trucks, buses, ships, and trains could, with some modification, run on liquid hydrogen, these modes of transportation could endure virtually in their present form if fossil-fuels become rare. The range of a jet could be doubled by conversion to liquid hydrogen.

Hydrogen becomes a liquid when compressed and cooled to −423°F (−253C). Of course, this cryogenic form of storage requires a subsystem capable of maintaining this low temperature. The available energy in liquid hydrogen approaches 2½ times the power of gasoline per unit weight. Hydrogen produces more energy per pound than any other fuel.

Another method, hydride storage, releases hydrogen when heated. This system is attractive because of its more normal, ambient storage temperatures. When a hydride storage system is used, storage takes up 50% more space than current gas tanks. There is also a 300-pound (136 kg) weight penalty, but this is offset by the normal storage temperatures. Hydride systems work when certain metals such as magnesium and titanium are fused with hydrogen. The hydride thus formed is then heated to release the hydrogen at a later time. Heat could be supplied partially by the engine exhaust to liberate the hydrogen. New hydride research is being conducted to help solve storage problems.

The most efficient use of hydrogen in an automobile would be the hydrogen-oxygen mixture which uses pure oxygen instead of air. Of course, an additional tank would have to be carried. This has always been a problem with hydrogen cars in general. The problem of storage is a fact that we must live with if we will ever see hydrogen cars as a reality in the future.

Because of the expense involved with hydrogen production, we may not see hydrogen automobiles in general use until the 21st Century. Progress in hydrogen-powered vehicles will be an interesting subject to follow in the years to come.

The main argument against the proliferation of hydrogen as a fuel is the fact that it becomes very expensive to produce. If electrolysis is used to electrically split water into hydrogen and oxygen, the application of large amounts of power is required. Producing hydrogen with the electrolysis process is an expensive method, therefore cheap, abundant electricity is needed. If the price of the electricity can be reduced or more efficient means of power perfected, hydrogen production on a large scale will be more feasible.

"On site" production of hydrogen from a power station could be accomplished with off-peak energy salvaging. Also, the construction of nuclear power plants in safe, remote areas such as deserts could produce fresh water and pure oxygen as by-products, while supplying hydrogen to our electric system.

It is possible that even with the energy conversion costs at both ends, a hydrogen pipeline may be cheaper to operate than conventional electric transmission lines.

Studies indicate that because hydrogen can store energy, it has a built-in advantage over power lines.

In 1970, eight million tons of hydrogen, or about three trillion standard cubic feet, were produced. The hydrogen produced is being used for ammonia production (42%), and petroleum refining (38%) plus uses for metallurgy and food processing.

Some people associate hydrogen with danger. Perhaps the most memorable event which precipitated this wary regard of hydrogen was the accident of the Zeppelin Hindenburg, which went up in flames in Lakehurst, New Jersey, in 1937. The Hindenburg used hydrogen to fill its gas bags for buoyancy.

Because hydrogen is the lightest element, risks of ignition can be less than gasoline because leaks will diffuse quickly in any ventilated area, reducing the potential of flame travel. If hydrogen is handled intelligently and care is taken to provide proper ventilation, and prevent causes of accidental ignition, then hydrogen is as safe as any other fuel we are presently using.

The Los Alamos Federal Test Facility conducted a test with a 500-gallon (1893 l) liquid hydrogen spill. It was observed that once in the gaseous state, hydrogen disperses into the atmosphere quickly and becomes harmless within 60 seconds. This is contrary to gasoline which, when spilled, collects in pools around an accident site, remaining a hazard for a long time. Even when completely mixed with air, hydrogen will not detonate unless it is compressed or ignited by a strong spark.

The basic building block of the hydrogen society in the immediate future will be the implementation of several existing concepts of energy production. These technologies all have one thing in common—they must face and conquer technical obstacles before they will be ac-

ceptable. All of us must cooperate to allow the breakthroughs of science and the participation of many nations to overcome technical barriers.

ALTERNATE SOURCES

A key factor in alternate energy development is how much attention world governments will devote to the subject. There are "ongoing" projects today, some of which are not fully functioning, economical or even well designed. Some are struggling first and second generation systems, that will provide valuable information for scientists, engineers, and designers to help third, fourth and fifth generation systems which may give us hard facts and solutions to major problems.

The aviation industry did not move from the Wright Brothers' airplane to the SST in one step; there were evolutionary processes that followed before a level of sophistication could be achieved. The opponents of alternate energy sources may ridicule their inefficiency or relatively low power output. But, in the future, when we must extract from this earth the power which we cannot obtain through fossil-fuels, their opinion will undoubtedly change.

Nuclear Fission

Today nuclear power generates about 3% of our electricity. By the year 2000 this may be increased to 50%. The thermal efficiency of nuclear reactors is about 33% for light water reactors and 40% for the experimental breeder reactors which actually produce more fuel than they consume.

The advantages of nuclear power are many. It is clean, has low pollution, is relatively safe, inexpensive, and quiet.

The disadvantages are centered around the potential hazards regarding the disposal of radioactive waste materials which remain deadly for as long as 250,000 years.

Coal

Coal-fired power generating plants now supply about 47% of our electricity. Modern coal-fired boilers are about 40% efficient. This compares quite favorably to the average automobile which has a 16% efficiency.

The advantages of coal are that there are several hundred years of reserves which will provide power for electricity *and* supply hydrocarbon derivatives which can replace oil and gas in the future.

Coal's disadvantages include the increasing costs of mining, problems with restoring mined areas, health hazards and costly "laundering" of high sulfur coals.

Solar Energy

Solar power is a continually-renewable energy source which has the greatest potential as an alternate to coal, gas, and oil. Solar power is clean and offers safe energy. Its disadvantages are related to economics. Presently, costs of all systems are high while efficiencies are low.

Wind Power

The energy extracted from wind is associated with solar energy because the wind blows as a result of the sun's effect upon air masses. Overall potential for wind power on a large scale remains quite low. However, this source of energy can be successfully adapted to private homes, small industries, and localities with favorable conditions.

Geothermal

Goethermal energy is power from the earth's molten core. Steam-powered generators convert the heat into electricity at about 20% efficiency. This method is used in several areas of the world. Unfortunately the areas where this energy may be extracted are limited. Also, possible dangers exist from potential earthquakes and land cave-ins.

Waste or Garbage Recycling

Because it is free, garbage is a cheap fuel. The use of waste to produce electricity provides power while disposing of an unwanted commodity. Benefits of waste recycling include the potential to produce synthetic oil and methane gas. Also, there is significant revenue acquired from recycling metals from garbage.

Flywheels and Other Storage Systems

The key to higher efficiencies from nuclear and hydroelectric power plants is "energy storage"—storing energy during periods of low demand, to be used at peak demand periods.

Because alternating current cannot be stored efficiently, it must be generated as it is used. Use of power is heavily concentrated during daytime business hours and thus power plants are idle at night. Storage of power generated at night would allow use during the day, minimizing requirements to build power plants and allow them to operate in a more efficient mode. The flywheel is one of man's oldest inventions and can provide an efficient method to store energy. Flywheels have a higher storage capacity than do batteries. A 200-ton flywheel designed for a power plant could achieve storage efficiencies of up to 95%.

Other storage systems include batteries of advanced design. Also, alternate methods use large reservoirs above a river or stream into which water is pumped during off hours to be extracted later when the demand is higher, to spin turbines and generate power.

Magnetohydrodynamics

Magnetohydrodynamics, or MHD, is a recent invention which is an alternative to conventional power station generators. In this system, a rocket exhaust containing conductive particles passes through a magnetic field, producing electricity with an efficiency potential of 60%. The fuel used can be oil, coal dust, or gas. The prime advantage of the system is that it has no moving parts. Development may provide MHD power plants capable of supplying electric power to the United States in the next decade.

The high efficiency of MHD power and other advantages over nuclear power, such as safety and less waste heat add to its attractiveness.

Hydrogen Fusion

Hydrogen fusion is the light at the end of the alternate energy tunnel. It is the source of power which causes the sun to radiate energy over the earth, and it is a major building block of the future.

Nuclear fusion is the result of fusing or combining the nuclei of atoms together—the opposite of nuclear fission which splits atoms apart to create energy.

The principal fuel for thermonuclear fusion is deuterium, a naturally occurring material found in sea water. There is enough deuterium in the oceans to supply energy for several million years, and it is infinitely more economical than uranium.

Thermonuclear fusion produces little or no radioactive wastes unlike fission which produces plutonium—a waste product that remains deadly for 250,000 years. Unfortunately, fusion must reach the break-even point before it can be used to generate power. Break-even is the point where the reactor can manufacture more power than it consumes.

The process of fusion consumes a great deal of power and requires a special set of circumstances to create the effect. Firstly, a deuterium fuel pellet must be raised to 100 million degrees and held at that temperature for up to 1 second. A container, which holds the superheated material called "plasma," is created by holding the atoms in a magnetic "bottle." The material is then compressed at a 10,000-to-one ratio to produce "ignition," the point at which fusion actually occurs.

Safety considerations for fusion are substantially less than nuclear fission. A fusion reactor cannot "run away" because the extremely difficult conditions necessary to create a reaction must be precisely maintained or ignition ceases.

The experimental fusion device which can achieve the break-even point may not be in operation until the 1980's. Because of the long time span necessary to develop a commercial power plant after the first fusion break even demonstration, we will probably not see fusion in commercial use until the 21st Century. This parallels the development of nuclear fission reactors which were demonstrated in 1942, yet did not become a practical reality until 1967.

There is no doubt that the aggregate total of man's technology will be required to effectively produce a successful hydrogen fusion reactor. Some sources indicate that it may be up to fifty years before we see one actually in use, producing electricity to be applied to our energy system. The time table will be contingent upon breakthroughs in development, technological advances and perhaps luck. One thing remains clear, however, that when and *if* hydrogen fusion becomes a reality, we will see an abundance of energy on earth.

THE PLACE OF THE ELECTRIC VEHICLE IN THE FUTURE

No one can paint with any accuracy an energy picture of the world in the year 2000. Trends indicate that the fossil fueled private and commercial vehicles may become rare or extinct in the 21st Century. The priority of petroleum products will be directed to more essential uses, such as the production of plastics and fertilizers.

The development of a totally electric, hydrogen economy seems attractive when considering the alternatives. In such a society, electric vehicles will contribute to conservation of fossil fuels. But, individual habits regarding energy waste must change before we can face some of the problems of the distant future.

The concept of vehicle rentals may take an unusual twist in the future. The average urban dweller could have one or two electric vehicles and rent a gasoline or hydrogen powered road vehicle for vacationing. The rented pleasure vehicle could be more luxurious than one could imagine, with onboard computer, entertainment, and recreational facililties. The cost of such a vehicle would be beyond the reach of the average person to own, but not to rent for a week. Therefore, we would see families both enjoying their vacations and conserving energy.

The rental concept may be taken to another extreme to include rental of both commuter vehicle and "battery time" used. Plastic, rubber and non-corroding metals could lead to rental vehicles which are exceptionally strong and long lived, to maximize investments.

Now that we have observed the vast potential for alternate power, it is easier to understand how electric vehicles enter into the overall picture of the future. Although the new uses of hydrogen as a combustible gasoline substitute will make possible the existence of such familiar modes of transportation as airplanes, trains, cross-country trucks, and oceangoing vessels, personal transportation will probably be dominated by electric vehicles.

Recent studies have been conducted to determine the effect a large number of electric vehicles would have upon the energy producing capabilities of utilities. These studies by electric companies did not show a significant increase necessary in the capacity requirements of today's utilities.

As an example, Chicago's Commonwealth Edison noted the difference between peak and night demands for electricity is about two million kilowatts. This power would be adequate to charge 500,000 electric vehicles during the evening hours. Two hundred thousand of these vehicles would be charged by a combination of nuclear power plants and newer fossil-fuel facilities owned by Commonwealth Edison. The off-peak load demand patterns of most utilities across the U.S. have a similar pattern. Off-peak energy use could support the majority or all of the electric vehicles we could possibly produce before the year 1990. A Federal Power Commission survey indicated that thirty eight million electric vehicles could be on the road by 1990, and if only half of those were produced, the annual consumption of electricity required would reach about fifty two million megawatt-hours a year. This is equivalent to about 1% of the total projected energy production from all sources in 1990. According to these studies, it would seem that there would be a sufficient amount of power for us in the foreseeable future.

Electric vehicles complement the hydrogen society in that they will act as storage reservoirs for off-peak nuclear power station production. And they will bear the task of moving large numbers of human beings from one place to another.

Electric production from all sources of power today will not be sufficient for the additional consumption of energy used in transportation, in tomorrow's totally "electric community." The alternate systems mentioned earlier will have to be implemented, at least to some degree, because there will be demands upon electricity tomorrow that we don't see today, such as increased residential heating.

THE ELECTRIC AUTOMOBILE, IMMEDIATE FUTURE—AN EXPERT OPINION

There are few men in the world today that possess more experience in electric vehicle design and development than does Robert McKee, president and founder of the McKee Engineering Corporation in Palatine, Illinois. McKee has experience in development and engineering design that began over sixteen years ago, and has developed vehicles ranging from Formula A and Can-Am designs to the Howmet Turbine Cars that currently hold six international records.

McKee Engineering has contributed a myriad of innovations to all forms of vehicle development. For over nine years, concentration has been directed toward electric vehicles. McKee is the pioneer of the backbone frame concept. In this system, the batteries are situated in the center of the vehicle, surrounded by frame members. This provides easy access to the batteries, which roll out on a tray. Several prototype models use this system, which permits battery exchanges in less than five mintues.

Globe-Union Endura

The "Endura" is a four-passenger fiberglass experimental prototype built by McKee Engineering for Globe-Union, Milwaukee, Wisconsin. Globe-Union, a major battery manufacturer, produces batteries under many trade names including Sears, Ford, Jeep, Caterpillar, NAPA, AMC, Interstate, Farm & Fleet, and Gibson.

The Endura carries 20 Globe-Union lead-acid electric vehicle batteries weighing a total of 1300 lbs (590 kg). A 25 hp series-wound DC motor with a rear-wheel-powered transaxle is regulated by a solid-state controller from the 120-volt battery pack.

The vehicle weighs 3,200 lbs (1,451 kg) and features a fiberglass shell with integral steel roll cage for strength. The chassis is lightweight aluminum with backbone frame to house batteries and provide a low center of gravity. A removable rear quarter panel converts the Endura from a 2 + 2 coupe into a station wagon.

Top speed is 60 mph (97 km/hr); acceleration is 0 to 30 mph (48 km/hr) in 8.7 seconds. Range is 115 miles at 35 mph (185 km at 56 km/hr).

Corporations such as ESB, Inc., (Electric Storage Battery Company), Barrett Electronics, Victor Comptometer, McCulloch, Westinghouse, Autodynamics, Electric Fuel Propulsion, Linear Alpha, and Globe Union have used the capable skills of McKee Engineering. In each case, the design and implementation of the prototype vehicle was suited to individual needs. McKee Engineering has designed, built, and tested more "on-road" experimental electric vehicles than any company in the United States. Because Bob McKee is eminently qualified to offer a prognosis of the future of transportation, I interviewed him on a number of pertinent subjects:

Q.   Will electric vehicles become part of future personal transportation?

McKee: I definitely think the answer is yes. The oil supply is finite. There are a lot better uses for it than using it up at a very rapid rate for transportation. We have to work toward other areas where we can, in effect, burn coal or use solar energy, hydroelectric or nuclear power for transportation, and the electric vehicle is the only way we can do that at the present time.

Q.   Is battery system technology a

MCKEE/GLOBE UNION "ENDURA"

Photo courtesy of McKee/Globe-Union

Photo courtesy of McKee/Globe-Union

Quick access to the 20 Globe Union electric vehicle batteries is made by removing front bumper assembly. The aluminum backbone frame houses a battery tray which uses rollers to provide battery removal.

The Endura uses a 25-hp series-wound DC motor mounted to a transaxle.

major stumbling block in the development of practical electric cars?

McKee: Everyone would like to see more powerful batteries, and this, of course, will come in due time. Today's batteries are subject to problems with regard to cold and corrosion. When the temperature drops to $-40°F$, $(-40C)$ battery power drops to zero. I feel that there is a way that the lead-acid battery will fulfill most of our requirements today. At least for the second car. With battery development progressing quite rapidly, the battery companies we have worked with are optimistic about improving the lead-acid battery significantly in the next ten years. There are also nickel-zinc batteries, lithium-sulphur, sodium-sulphur, zinc-chlorine, and a host of more exotic batteries further down the road. As far as fuel cells which use hydrogen or other fuels, I feel that most of their popularity has somewhat died down in recent years.

Q. How far are we from optimum motor technology?

McKee: New motors keep improving as new materials are available. There really has never been a need to make a more efficient motor in most cases except for aircraft applications. Motors today are from 35% to 70% efficient. Some of the motors we are using in electric cars are quite efficient and, without much expense, could be even better. When there is more need for an efficient motor, people will work on it and it will become available.

Q. How important is streamlining in an electric vehicle?

McKee: You have to keep the frontal area low and eliminate as many protuberances as possible. The use of flush mounted glass and NASA's minimum-drag air inlets can also be helpful. The technique of incorporating a belly pan into the design also helps because the first two-thirds of the vehicle are critical.

The Sundancer car which has been given extreme streamlining attention requires only 23 pounds of pull to keep it moving along at 30 mph. There was also an effort to reduce mechanical drag in the Sundancer by eliminating packed wheel bearings. Here we used ten-weight spindle oil and magnetic seals to cut down drag.

Q. What are your feelings on electric vehicle braking systems?

McKee: We have used drum brakes or hydraulic disc brakes with pad retractors to reduce drag. We have also constructed vehicles with regenerative braking. Claims of up to 12% improved range have been made in this area—but there still are some problems. When the road speed is too high, batteries will receive more power than they can cope with. When the road speed is too low, power retrieved becomes inadequate. The controller in such a system becomes complicated. I feel a good variable-speed transmission would make regenerative braking more feasible.

Q. How do you go about heating an electric vehicle?

McKee: We scavenge the waste heat from the motor and controller as much as possible, but that is not adequate for a midwestern winter. The use of a support system fossil-fuel heater will help heat the vehicle as well as the batteries on extremely cold days. Higher battery temperatures result in higher efficiencies.

Q. What has been your experience with electric vehicle maintenance?

McKee: Maintenance is one of the areas where electric vehicles prove outstanding. The life of an electric is double or triple that of the internal combusion engine car, and maintenance is comparatively minimal. And, of course, there are no anti-pollution controls to require attention.

Because electronic control for electric vehicles is relatively new, particularly the SCR, there can be maintenance problems with these components. The problems, however, are being solved.

Our experience with the ESB Sundancer showed that, after 6,000 miles of combined stop-and-go and high-speed driving, the only maintenance required was a grease job and a new set of brake pads. This vehicle did not exhibit any mechanical problems.

Q. What is the potential of a hybrid vehicle?

McKee: The hybrid vehicle is the solution for certain applications that would need an extended range beyond that of a pure electric car. The vehicle itself, of course, becomes more complicated. If you use an internal combustion engine (diesel or gasoline) or, for that matter, any variety of heat engine, the vehicle becomes complicated. Consideration must be given to emission controls and generally the vehicle would be more expensive. This extra expense could be justified for buses and certain other applications where there are enough miles on the road to justify the additional cost and complications.

Q. What do you think of the flywheel for future transportation?

McKee: A flywheel is a beautiful way to store energy, particularly when your vehicle is being stopped, because energy can be regenerated and used to speed up the flywheel. This energy can then be used for acceleration. The biggest problem is the transmission. An infinitely-variable-speed transmission is the most desirable solution. A flywheel is particularly suited for start-and-stop driving and for applications that require a high-peak power which can be stored as energy in a flywheel.

Lockheed Aerospace and others have worked with flywheels. Carbon filaments have been used in flywheel compositon as well as

4340 steel. There are good arguments for both; I feel at this time that it is simpler to use a non-superflywheel which is in the range of 10,000 RPM rather than 35,000 RPM. The higher-speed version has to run in a vacuum with magnetic drive through the case and becomes extremely expensive and complicated for electric vehicle application.

For postal service operation the lower-speed version could easily increase the useable range.

Q. What do you think the role of the hydrogen car will be in the future?

McKee: There have been a lot of people working on the hydrogen car. Hydrogen certainly burns cleanly and when you burn it, you have water as an emission. Of course, hydrogen is extremely explosive and I feel small leaks can be the basis of concern. A gas leak is one of the potential problems with a butane or propane vehicle. The small leak can fill up the trunk or interior of the car, and that is potentially dangerous. We haven't really been involved in propane or hydrogen-powered vehicles—but we have produced race cars which run at Indianapolis on methanol and nitro-methane and fire is a real hazard. This, of course, is an extreme application.

I don't see that safety is the major stumbling block for the hydrogen car. I feel it is, instead, how to produce the quantities of hydrogen necessary.

Q. What projects have you been working on for your clients?

McKee: We built an electric vehicle for Westinghouse as a test bed for some of their components. Most of our customers are manufacturers of components such as batteries, motors, and controllers. Some of the vehicles have not been released for publicity because they are strictly research oriented. One vehicle we built for McCulloch, the chain saw manufacturer, was a 96-inch (245 cm) wheel base vehicle, which was about the size of a Corvette. We built two cars for ESB, which were called the Sundancer, a small commuter car, and recently finished a car for Globe Union Company, manufacturer of the Sears DieHard batteries. This car, called the Endura, is a four-passenger vehicle with a 60-mph (96 km/hr) top speed and 135-mile (217 km) range at 35 mph (56 km/hr).

Q. How much would the Globe Union Endura cost, if produced?

McKee: If manufactured by General Motors or Ford, for example, it would be comparable in price to the cars they are now producing. Automobile production is very volume-sensitive. The more you make of them, the cheaper they get in a hurry.

Q. Why do you think GM or Ford isn't pushing electric vehicle production?

McKee: They are building vehicles for which a market exists. There is no market yet for an electric vehicle. I feel it will be a few years before people in the United States will be ready to buy a low-performance automobile such as an electric car.

To better understand the problem of introducing a new automobile, one must understand the process. Generally, it takes about seven years from the idea stage to the production of an automobile. If you're going to produce a car in seven years, you have to be thinking about it right now. If we had a crash program, perhaps we would accomplish the task in half the time, but remember, federal regulations on safety and product liability that exist today cause a reluctance to jump into the market until there is some assurance that all of the problems are cured. It seems to me that it may be quite a while before a big company in this country is going to commit itself wholeheartedly to this project.

Analyze what is happening today. Automobiles are shrinking in size each year. A number of years ago a Ford Pinto was a very small car—a subcompact. Now it's an average size car and the Ford Fiesta is a subcompact. In the future, we will be driving smaller cars, because gas is going up and there is a mandated mileage requirement. The easiest way to reach these goals is to decrease the frontal area and reduce the vehicle weight, and make it more streamlined. This is the direction in which cars are headed.

I think that Detroit is taking a more serious look into electric cars, with Ford working on the sodium-sulphur battery, and General Motors proceeding with ongoing programs. Ten years ago, GM made a few prototypes, but no long-term commitments.

In the future, it is conceivable that large gasoline-powered cars may not be allowed in the inner city. Right now at peak rush hours, pollutants rise above the EPA's recommended amounts. I feel that there is a need for better mass transportation that will attract passengers and help reduce automotive use. Smaller cars will help, as will car pools. Politically, if oil-producing nations would stop exporting one day, electric cars would then look much more attractive.

Q. Do you think Japan will be the first country to market an effective electric automobile?

McKee: They certainly have more government funding for electric vehicle development and of course they have a major pollution problem. Because they have to import all of their fuel, they have the incentive to work on electric cars. Many of their large corporations are spending money on this project. In many cases, the vehicles they have produced were a joint effort. One company will produce the mechani-

McKEE "SUNDANCER"

Photo courtesy of McKee Engineering

cal parts, a battery company will supply components, and motors and controls will be supplied by another company. This, then, will be funded by the Japanese government and a test vehicle will result. They have a good head start, considering there has been work on this type of vehicle for years. Also, their economy lends itself more toward the acceptance of smaller cars.

Q.   If there was a suitable electric automobile produced today, would you consider owning one?

McKee: The electric would make a fine second car and would probably serve 95% of my needs. I live within five miles of the office and that would be fine for commuting.

McKee SUNDANCER

The "Sundancer" is an experimental, two passenger prototype built by McKee Engineering,

Palatine, Illinois, U.S.A., for the ESB Corporation, Philadelphia, Pennsylvania. ESB (Electric Storage Battery), a major battery manufacturer totally committed to the advancement of battery and electric vehicle technology, commissioned the construction of two Sundancers to

Photo courtesy of McKee Engineering

SUNDANCER BACKBONE FRAME

Mr. Robert McKee, president of McKee Engineering, demonstrates the operation of the Sundancer's front-loading battery tray. A fresh set of batteries can be installed in less than five minutes.

The backbone frame, a McKee innovation, allows for a low center of gravity and isolates batteries from the car's occupants.

serve as test beds for batteries, controllers and motors.

Features of the Sundancer are: rear mounted 8 hp motor with two speed transaxle, fiberglass body and backbone frame with front loading battery tray.

Top speed is 60 miles per hour (96 km/hr); range is 80 miles (130 km) city and 120 miles (193 km) at a steady 30 mph (48 km/hr). Acceleration is 0 to 30 mph (48 km/hr) in 9 seconds. Weight is 1600 lbs (725 kg) of which 850 lbs (386 kg) is batteries.

MASS TRANSPORTATION OF THE FUTURE

There are some people who take a dim view of mass transportation in general. They feel the majority of cities, such as Los Angeles, are not suitable for mass transportation to begin with. In some regards, their arguments sound valid; the majority of people would prefer to own their own automobiles over other methods of transportation. The autonomy and freedom a private vehicle offers cannot be matched by even the most sophisticated mass transportation system.

Our modern highway systems, which are a means of transporting millions of human beings from one place to another, can also be thought of as mass transportation. The automobile, considered part of that system, after all, does serve the masses.

It may also be true that even if the electric trains, monorails, buses, or subways were subsidized by the government to the point that they were absolutely free to all users, it is doubtful the conventional automobile would be endangered. The freedom of mobility that Americans have enjoyed is one which will not be relinquished easily. To be able to come and go as one pleases is in many instances a justification for the private vehicle that even a price of $2.00 per U.S. gallon would fail to deter.

Therefore, we must consider the small electric urban automobile integrated into a partially automated highway system, as a real life example of mass transportation.

Undoubtedly the highway systems of the world are one of man's most impressive accomplishments, surely to be compared with the other great wonders of the world. The highway conglomerate that we have created unfortunately blocks efforts for a truly efficient mass transportation system that would serve our needs in the future. As cities encroach upon each other's space, the suburbs of one city will become the suburbs of its neighboring city. Then perhaps we may see a greater potential for efficient urban transportation systems.

The high death and injury rate on our highways is further proof that a better solution is desirable. The inefficient use of our present mass transportation in urban areas doubly creates a need for a better solution. Trains and rapid transit units sit dormant during non-rush hour periods or are overused in rush hour periods to the point of making them undesirable for human conditions. The seeds we have sown in our devotion to building a secure place for the automobile and truck bears bitter fruit. Our railroads are deteriorating and are in financial difficulty. The simple gasoline buggy of a past era is now a seven thousand dollar well padded and soundproof device within which we may kill ourselves. Our highways require maintenance, taxes, and were built when gasoline was an inexpensive commodity. Those conditions have changed.

Man enjoys his "freedom of mobility," which is the basic reason why automobiles are so prevalent today. It may be difficult to construct completely automated highways, which take the driving responsibilities out of the control of the driver. A semi-automatic highway which has one automated lane for those who do not wish to be encumbered by driving, may be a more realistic approach. On the automated lane, the cars can be spaced closer together and safely carry a larger number of vehicles.

The fully automated automobile that would tell you where you're going, how long it will take to get there, how much gasoline it will consume at a specified speed, and have the ability to park itself, is really not too far fetched.

The 1978 Cadillac Seville incorporates an optional micro computer. Presently its duties are limited to calculating trips and distances travelled in their relationship to projected gas mileage based upon the fuel monitored through the fuel injection system. Also, the unit displays the time, engine speed, and the gasoline consumption at a given speed. This is the first step toward a real "thinking" system to be installed in an automobile to date. Surely, a stepping stone in the direction that vehicles will be approaching in the next decade.

Eventually, a micro computer will control all aspects of engine control, accessories, instrumentation, time keeping and entertainment.

Photo courtesy of Bay Area Rapid Transit District

THE BAY AREA RAPID TRANSIT (BART)

The Bay Area Rapid Transit connects Oakland to San Francisco, California through a 75 mile (120 km) highly automated system. This electric railway uses over 450 cars, which are built by Rohr, and have fully automated computer controlled capability.

The BART network features 14 subway, 13 aerial, and 7 surface stations. One engineering feat includes the 4 mile transbay tube buried up to 135′ (40 m) underwater.

The cars are powered by a third rail 1000-volt DC propulsion system. One 150-hp motor per axle, four motors per car can allow an 80 mph (129 km/hr) maximum speed. The normal trip is 39 mph (63 km/hr) average, including 20-second station stops. Acceleration and deceleration is 3 mph (4.8 km/hr) per second maximum.

The system uses a totally automated computerized control manufactured by Westinghouse. Manual operation can override computer operation with onboard controls. To date BART has served over one hundred million patrons and has registered over 1.5 billion passenger miles (2.4 billion km).

We may speculate on various topics such as: totally automated vehicles which can be programmed to drive passengers to specific destinations, park themselves, recharge and return upon command.

The manifestations of space-age transportation may reveal themselves in new forms which we have not as yet imagined. The comfort and technological conveniences incorporated into 21st Century transportation may indeed be lavish. The Buck Rogers concept of the world which we have long awaited, may yet arrive. But, until we can devise a system such as one which disassociates mass and reassociates it in another place, we are saddled with the prospect of physically moving people and goods. So, let us bring our discussion of "vehicles of the future" down to the terrestrial, and leave science fiction for a while.

Today, we see progress being made in giant steps in subminiature electronics, micro-processers and technology of a truly advanced society.

Investment will have to be made in urban and highway systems to meet the needs of electric vehicles. Highways will have to provide a special lane or "power strips" to allow high speed electric vehicle use which would effectively increase range and performance. City streets will have to be constructed in a similar manner and vehicle owners charged for energy consumed. Charging stations will begin as an adjunct to regular service stations. Battery packs will be exchanged and owned by manufacturers. When the battery system has reached the end of its useful life, the manufacturer will recycle the components, minimizing the power required to build new batteries.

No one can say if we will see underground highways, double, triple and quadruple decked highways—or any highways at all. Perhaps a reconstruction of urban housing will attract suburban dwellers back to the inner-city. They can be remodeled, refurbished, and even made attractive by rent subsidies.

Some considerations for the mass transportation of the future include moving sidewalks, or people-moving devices, or totally automated minibuses that could be programmed to stop at certain points by the passengers. These suggestions are directed to the task of moving people from one place to another. There may be a trend to move places from person to person.

It is absurd to see a woman use a 4,000 pound car to go three miles to purchase a bag of groceries. Perhaps we should eliminate the necessity for this trip altogether. An in-home minicomputer could be connected to the neighborhood supermarket. The woman could code in the required groceries, to be dispatched to her by electric delivery van. The purchase would be billed directly to her bank account. The use of large, centralized supermarket warehouses could even eliminate the need for a neighborhood supermarket altogether.

When one stops to consider the total fuel use related to driving to and from work, non-essential shopping, and frivolous waste, it is easy to see where we can reduce our overall oil consumption by a significant amount without endangering the quality of life to which we are accustomed.

The use of moving lunch wagons could service large office buildings in downtown areas. Car pools for large companies could get groups of people to work in one vehicle.

By bringing the services to the home we can eliminate fuel used for transportation. The trend toward the static rather than the mobile form of communication may enable us to even further compartmentalize ourselves in our daily life.

It is conceivable that a person's occupation could be conducted in the comfort of his own home. If micro-processers that could interconnect both home and office are employed, there would be little need to deliver the employee twenty miles or so to work, when work could be merely an extension of his own home environment. If a salesman desired to call upon a client, the sale could be negotiated as easily via a videophone or holographic (three-dimensional illusion) image that would enable him to call upon many prospects in a day versus merely a few.

The necessity to travel great distances, and consume large quantities of fuel in the process, to visit one's relatives across the country, may also be eliminated by holographic conference rooms, situated in large metropolitan communication centers. Real-life illusions of a family meeting with people present from various cities at one time in one room with cross conversations and absolute realism, may negate the need for unnecessary travel.

Let us be concerned with the end product before we devote our energies to an antiquated concept. Surely, the steam driven train of the turn of the century was considered a technical marvel, one which the average layman would be hard pressed to improve. Yet the airplane and trucking industry have devastated the railroads.

Future generations may view the antiquated gesticulation of the internal combustion engine as a humorous side-note to a misguided era of man's development which relied upon primitive fuels, producing outrageous energy consumption, pollution, and wastefulness.

In the future, every factory or office building roof will be equipped with solar cells for collectors to accumulate energy. In heavy metropolitan areas, the surface area of a roof approaches or approximates the ground area. This space is totally ignored. We must trim down the waste, so that we may enjoy our lives in a cleaner and more efficient manner—not to make us automatons—but to allow us to live clean, healthy and productive lives in a streamlined, wasteless society.

Some day the outmoded concept of getting from one place to another could quite possibly be replaced by "traveling" via holographic image, at the speed of light, 186,000 miles per second (299,000 km/sec). Is this the ultimate interpretation of transportation in the future?

Directory of Select Electric Vehicle Associations and Clubs

American Public Power Association
2600 Virginia Avenue, N.W.
Washington, D.C. 20037
USA

Battery Council International
111 East Wacker Drive
Chicago, Illinois 60601
USA

Copper & Brass Information Center
North House, 321 Kent Street
Sydney, N.S.W. 2000
AUSTRALIA

Copper Development Association, Inc.
405 Lexington Avenue
New York, N.Y. 10017
USA

Denver Electric Vehicle Council
Route 3, Box 700
Golden, Colorado 80401
USA

Electric Auto Association
1674 Merrill Drive, No. 12
San Jose, Calif. 95124
USA

Electric Power Research Institute
P.O. Box 10412
Palo Alto, Calif. 94303
USA

Electric Vehicle Association Of Great Britain, Ltd.
30 Millbank
London, SW1P4RD
ENGLAND

Electric Vehicle Association Of Ohio
2060 Arthur Avenue
Lakewood, Ohio 44107
USA

Electric Vehicle Council
90 Park Avenue
New York, N.Y. 10016
USA

Independent Battery Manufacturers Association, Inc.
100 Larchwood Drive
Largo, Florida 33540
USA

Institute Of Electrical & Electronics Engineers
345 East 47th Street
New York, N.Y. 10017
USA

International Lead Zinc Research Organization, Inc.
292 Madison Avenue
New York, N.Y. 10017
USA

Japan Automobile Manufacturing Association
4-1 Chome Otemachi, Chiyoda-Ku
Tokyo
JAPAN

Japan Electric Association
3-1 Chome Yuraku-Cho, Chiyoda-Ku
Tokyo
JAPAN

Japan Lead Zinc Development Association
No. 1-3-6 Uchisalwaicho, Chiyoda-Ku
Tokyo
JAPAN

Lead Development Association
34 Berkeley Square
London W1X 6AJ
ENGLAND

Lead Industries Association, Inc.
292 Madison Avenue
New York, N.Y. 10017
USA

Motor Vehicle Manufacturers Assn. Of U.S.
320 New Center Building
Detroit, Michigan 48202
USA

National Electrical Manufacturers Association
155 E. 44th Street
New York, N.Y. 10017
USA

New Zealand Battery Electric Vehicle Club
14 Hospital Road
Kawakawa
NEW ZEALAND

Scandinavian Lead Zinc Association
22 Sturegatan
Stockholm
SWEDEN

Society Of Automotive Engineers, Inc.
400 Commonwealth Dr.
Warrendale, Pa. 15096
USA

Unipede
39 Avenue de Friedland
75008 Paris
FRANCE

U.S. Dept. of Energy
Electric and Hybrid Vehicle Systems
Transportation Energy Conservation
Washington, D.C. 20245
USA

This list was extracted from a directory prepared by the ELECTRIC VEHICLE NEWS

Manufacturers of Electric Vehicle Related Products

AM General Corporation
32500 Van Born Road
Wayne, Michigan 48184
USA

Accumulatorenfabrik
Sonnenschein GmbH
Thiergarten
D-6470 Buedingen/Hessen
GERMANY

Accumulatorenfabriken
Wilhelm Hagen AG
Thomastr, 27/28
477 Soest
GERMANY

Accumulatorenwerk Hoppecke
Carl Zoellner & Sohn
Barbarossaplatz 2
D-5000 Koln 1
WEST GERMANY

Amback Industries Incorporated
American Bosch Electrical
Products Div.
P.O. Box 2228
Columbus, Miss. 39701
USA

American-Lincoln, Div. of the Scott & Fetzer Co.
1100 Haskins Rd.
Bowling Green, Ohio 43402
USA

AMIGO Inc.
6693 Dixie Highway
Bridgeport, Michigan 48722
USA

Anker Batterier a.s.
P.O. Box 25
3191 Horten
NORWAY

Applied Motors, Inc.
P.O. Box 106
Rockford, Ill. 61105
USA

Asser Transportmiddelen Fabriek B.V.
Dr. A. F. Philipsweg 13
Assen
NETHERLANDS

B & Z Electric Car
3346 Olive Avenue
Signal Hill, Calif.
USA

Battronic Truck Corp.
Third & Walnut Sts.
Boyertown, Pa. 19512
USA

Bendix Corp., Automotive Control Systems Group
401 Bendix Drive
South Bend, Indiana 46624
USA

Berix Electric AB
Box 3015
S-462 03 Vanersborg
SWEDEN

Big Joe Manufacturing Co.
7225 N. Kostner Ave.
Chicago, Ill. 60646
USA

The Boeing Co. — Vertol Div.
P.O. Box 16858,
Philadelphia, Pa. 19142
USA

Robert Bosch Corporation
2800 South 25th Ave.
Broadview, Illinois 60153
USA

Brubaker Group
10315 W. Pico Blvd.
Los Angeles, California 90064
USA

Centron Systems, Inc.
4501 Maryland
St. Louis, Mo. 63108
USA

Chloride Group Limited
52 Grosvenor Gardens
London SW1W OAU
ENGLAND

Chloride, Inc.
P.O. Box 24598
Tampa, Florida 33623
USA

Chloride Industrial Batteries
P.O. Box 15060
Kansas City, Kansas 66115
USA

Chloride Industrial Batteries Ltd.
10 Snitterton Road
Matlock, Derbyshire DE4 3L7
ENGLAND

Clark Equipment Co. — Industrial Truck Div.
24th & Lafayette Sts.
Battle Creek, Mich. 49016
USA

Corbin-Gentry, Inc.
40 Maple Street
Somersville, Connecticut 06072
USA

Coventry Climax Ltd.
Widdrington Rd.
Coventry CV1 4DX
ENGLAND

Cushman-Outboard Marine Corp.
P.O. Box 82409
Lincoln, Neb. 68501
USA

Daimler-Benz AG
Postfach 202
7 Stuttgart 60
GERMANY

Dana Corporation
Spicer Clutch Division
P.O. Box 191
Auburn, Indiana 46706
USA

John Deere Company
Moline, Illinois 61265
USA

Die Mesh Corporation
629 Fifth Avenue
Pelham, New York 10803
USA

ESB Incorporated
5 Penn Center Plaza
Philadelphia, Pa. 19103
USA

EVA/Chloride Corp.
9100 Bank Street
Cleveland, Ohio 44125
USA

E-Z-GO
P.O. Box 388
Augusta, Georgia 30903
USA

Eagle-Picher Industries, Inc.
P.O. Box 47
Joplin, Missouri 64801
USA

Eaton Corporation
11000 Roosevelt Blvd.
Philadelphia, Pa. 19115
USA

ElecTraction
Heybridge Basin
Maldon, Essex
ENGLAND

Electric Auto Corporation
2237 Elliott Avenue
Troy, Michigan 48084
USA

Electric Fuel Propulsion Corp.
Robbins Executive Park East
2191 Elliott Avenue
Troy, Michigan 48084
USA

Electric Passenger Cars, Inc.
5127 Galt Way
San Diego, California 92117
USA

Electric Vehicle Associates, Inc.
9100 Bank St.
Cleveland, Ohio 44125
USA

Electricar Corporation
P.O. Box 698
Norwalk, Connecticut 06852
USA

Energy Development Associates
1100 W. Whitcomb Ave.
Madison Heights, Michigan 48071
USA

Exxon Enterprises
P.O. Box 45
Linden, New Jersey 07036
USA

Fabbrica Accumulatori Uranio SpA
Corso Milano 88
37100 Verona
ITALY

Fabbrica Italiana Magneti Marelli SpA.
20099 Setso S. Giovanni
Milano
ITALY

Fabrica Espanola Magnetos, S.A.
Spartado 35005
Madrid-17
SPAIN

FIAT
Corso Marconi 10
Turin
ITALY

GES mbH
Tersteegenstrasse 77
4 Dusseldorf 30
GERMANY

The Garrett Corporation,
9851 Sepulveda Blvd.,
Los Angeles, Calif. 90009
USA

General Electric Co.
2000 Taylor St.
Fort Wayne, Ind. 46804
USA

General Electric Company
1501 Roanoke Blvd.
Salem, Va. 24153
USA

Globe-Union, Inc.
5757 N. Greenbay Ave.
Milwaukee, Wisc. 53201
USA

Gottfried Hagen AG
Rolshoverstrasse 95-101
5000 Cologne 91
WEST GERMANY

Gould, Inc.
30 Gould Center
Rolling Meadows, Illinois 60008
USA

Gulf & Western Industries, Inc.
1 Gulf & Western Plaza
New York, N.Y. 10023
USA

HB Electrical Mfg. Co., Inc.
P.O. Box 1466
Mansfield, Ohio 44901
USA

HB Switchgear (Contactors) Ltd.
Ipswich Road
Cardiff CF3 7XP, Wales
UNITED KINGDOM

Harbilt Electric Vehicles Ltd.
Rockingham Road
Market Harborough
Leicestershire LE16 7PU
ENGLAND

Huber Engineering Co.
P.O. Box 17
Galva, Illinois 61434
USA

Hunter Manufacturing Co.
30525 Aurora Road
Cleveland (Solon), Ohio 44139
USA

Hyster Company
P.O. Box 2902
Portland, Oregon 97208
USA

INACEL
Cornelio Saavedra 2720-Munro
Byebis Auresm
ARGENTINA

Japan Storage Battery Co. Ltd.
Kisshoin, Minami-ku
Kyoto
JAPAN

Jet Industries, Inc.
4201 South Congress
Austin, Texas 78745
USA

Johns-Manville Sales Corp.
P.O. Box 5108
Denver, Colorado 80217
USA

Kady-Kart Incorporated
20 Wilbraham Road
Palmer, Massachusetts 01069
USA

Kalamazoo Manufacturing Co.
1827 Reed Street
Kalamazoo, Michigan 49001
USA

Kaylor Energy Products
1918 Menatto Ave.
Menlo Park, California 94025
USA

King Engineering
5436 Topsfield Lane
Clay, New York 13041
USA

Lansing Bagnall, Ltd.
Kingsclere Road
Basingstoke, Hampshire RG21 2XJ
ENGLAND

Lucas Industries Limited
Great King Street
Birmingham B19 2XF
ENGLAND

McKee Engineering Corporation
411 West Colfax Street
Palatine, Illinois 60067
USA

Marathon Electric Vehicles Ltd.
8305 Le Creusot St.
Montreal H1P 2A2, Quebec
CANADA

Mawdsley's Ltd.
Dursley
Gloucestershire GL11 5AE
ENGLAND

Melex U.S.A., Inc.
1201 Front St., Suite 210
Raleigh, North Carolina 27609
USA

Newton Aids Ltd.
2-A Conway Street
London W4P 5HE
ENGLAND

Nissan Motor Co. Ltd.
1, Natsushima-Cho
Yokosuka
JAPAN

Oldham & Son Ltd.
Denton
Manchester M34 3AT
ENGLAND

Palmer Industries
P.O. Box 707, Union Station
Endicott, New York 13760
USA

Pargo, Inc.
P.O. Box 5544
Charlotte, North Carolina 28225
USA

Pedal Power Div.
General Engines, Inc.
591 Mantua Blvd.
Sewell, New Jersey
USA

Progetti Gestioni Ecologiche SpA
30099 S. Pietro Di Stra.
Venezia
ITALY

Rockwell International
Atomics Int'n'l. Div.
8900 DeSoto Avenue
Canoga Park, Calif. 91304
USA

Gianni Rogliatti
Cas Post 116
Turin
ITALY

S.A. Accumulateurs TUDOR
5981 Florival
Archennes
BELGUIM

SAEM
via Mentana 16
Monza (Milano)
ITALY

**S.A.F.T. (Societe des Accumulateurs
Fixes et de Traction)**
119 Avenue de President Wilson
Levallois-Perret 92300
FRANCE

SGL Batteries Manufacturing Co.
14650 Dequindre
Detroit, Michigan 48212
USA

Sebring-Vanguard, Inc.
Sebring Industrial Park
Sebring, Fla. 33870
USA

Smith's Electric Vehicles Limited
P.O. Box No. 6, Marquisway,
Team Valley Trading Estate
Gateshead, County Durham NE8 1YT
ENGLAND

**Sociedad Espanola del Acumulador
Tudor, S.A.**
Gaztambide, 49
Madrid, 15
SPAIN

SOVEL S.A.
164 Rue Leon Blum
69608 Villeurbanne
FRANCE

Spykstaal B.V.
P.O. Box 9
Spijkenisse
NETHERLANDS

Stewart Warner Corporation
South Wind Division
1514 Drover Street
Indianapolis, Indiana 46221
USA

Texas Instruments, Inc.
34 Forest Street
Attleboro, Massachusetts 02703
USA

Toyo-Kogyo Co. Ltd.
3-1, Shinchi, Fuchu-cho
Aki-Gun, Hiroshima
JAPAN

Toyota Motor Sales Company, Inc.
No. 3, 2-Chome Kudan, Chiyoda-Ku
Tokyo
JAPAN

Transitron
745 Fort Street
Honolulu, Hawaii 96813
USA

Triad Services, Inc.
10611 Haggerty Street
Dearborn, Michigan 48126
USA

Trojan Battery Co.
9440 Ann St.
Santa Fe Springs, Calif. 90670
USA

University of South Florida
College of Engineering
Fowler Avenue
Tampa, Florida 33620
USA

VARTA Batterie AG
Am Leineufer 51, Postfach 210540
D-3000 Hannover 21
GERMANY

VARTA Batteries Ltd.
Industrial Division
5000 Francios Cusson
Lachine
Quebec H8T 1B3
CANADA

Volkswagen Werk AG
Abteilungsleiter Forschung 6
318 Wolfsburg
GERMANY

W. & E. Vehicles
Harlescott
Shrewbury SY1 3AE
ENGLAND

C.H. Waterman Industries
White Pond Road
Athol, Massachusetts 01331
USA

White Materials Handling
130 Ninth Avenue South
Hopkins, Minn. 55343
USA

Yardney Electric Corporation
82 Mechanic Street
Pawcatuck, Connecticut 02891
USA

Yuasa Battery Co., Ltd.
Josai-cho, Takatsuki
Osaka
JAPAN

BIBLIOGRAPHY

BOOKS

CYCLOPEDIA OF AUTOMOBILE ENGINEERING
Chicago, American Technical Society, 1915.

Anderson, Edwin P.
ELECTRIC MOTORS
4300 W. 62nd St., Indianapolis, Ind. 46206,
Theodore Audel & Co., 1968.

Bergere, Thea.
AUTOMOBILES OF YESTERYEAR
New York, Dodd, Mead & Co., 1962.

Bishop, Calvin C.
FUNDAMENTALS OF ELECTRICITY
New York, N.Y., Chiton Company Books, 1960.

Bishop, Denis and Marshall, Prince
TRUCKS AND VANS 1897-1927
New York, The MacMillan Co., 1972.

Prepared by the *Bureau of Naval Personnel*
BASIC ELECTRICITY
New York, Dover Publications.

Butterworth, W. E.
WHEELS AND PISTONS: THE STORY OF
THE AUTOMOBILE
New York, Four Winds Press, 1971.

DiCerto, Joseph J.
THE ELECTRIC WISHING WELL: THE SOLUTION
TO THE ENERGY CRISIS
New York, Collier Books, 1976.

Donovan, Frank
WHEELS FOR A NATION
Thomas Y. Crowell Company, 1965.

Ewers, William I.
SOLAR ENERGY: A BIASED GUIDE
Northbrook, Ill., DOMUS Books, 1977.

Flink, James J.
AMERICA ADOPTS THE AUTOMOBILE 1895-1910.
London, England, Cambridge, Mass., The MIT Press,
1970.

Georgano, G. N.
THE COMPLETE ENCYCLOPEDIA OF MOTORCARS
1885 TO THE PRESENT
New York, E. P. Dutton & Co., Inc., 1968, 1972.

Jamison, Andrew
THE STEAM-POWERED AUTOMOBILE
Bloomington, London, Indiana University Press,
1975.

Karolevitz, Robert F.
THIS WAS PIONEER MOTORING
Seattle, Wash., Superior Publishing Co., 1968.

Lewis, Albert L. and Musciano, Walter A.
AUTOMOBILES OF THE WORLD
New York, Simon and Schuster, 1977.

Mantell, Charles L.
BATTERIES AND ENERGY SYSTEMS
New York, McGraw-Hill, 1970.

Nicholson, T. R.
PASSENGER CARS 1863-1904
855 Third Ave., New York, The MacMillan Co., 1970.

Ruchlis, Hyman
THE WONDER OF ELECTRICITY
49 E. 33rd Street, New York, N.Y., Harper & Row,
1965.

Scheel, J. D.
CARS OF THE WORLD IN COLOR
New York, E. P. Dutton & Co., Inc., 1963.

Edited By: *Schroeder, Jr., Joseph J.*
THE WONDERFUL WORLD OF AUTOMOBILES
1885-1930
Northfield, Ill., DBI Books, Inc., 1971.

Waard, John De and Klein, Aaron E.
ELECTRIC CARS
New York, Doubleday & Co., Inc., 1977.

Wellman, William R.
ELEMENTARY ELECTRICITY
450 W. 33rd St., New York, N.Y., 10001, Van
Nostrand Reinhold Co., 1971.

MISCELLANEOUS

ENCYCLOPEDIA AMERICANA 1978, Vol. 2 p. 815.

U.S. Department of Energy Report
"ELECTRIC & HYBRID VEHICLE PROGRAM"
EHV/Quarterly Report Vol. 2 No. 1, January, 1978.

U.S. Department of Energy Report
Public Law 94-413
The Electric & Hybrid Vehicle Research,
Development & Demonstration Act of 1976.
ELECTRIC & HYBRID VEHICLE PROGRAM,
December, 1977.

VAN NOSTRAND'S SCIENTIFIC ENCYCLOPEDIA
Fifth Edition 1976.

MAGAZINE ARTICLES

"ATHOL'S ANSWER TO THE ENERGY CRISIS"
Car and Driver (Oct. 1973) p. 72.

"CADILLAC'S COCKPIT COPILOT: TRIPMASTER"
Motor Trend (October, 1977) p. 106

"CARS AND KILOWATTS"
IEEE Spectrum (Nov. 1977) p. 65.

"THE COMING HYDROGEN ECONOMY"
Fortune (Nov. 1972) p. 138.

"DC NOW, AC LATER?"
Machine Design (Oct. 17, 1974) p. 129.

Electric Vehicle News:
Feb., May, August, Nov.—1974
Feb., May, August, Nov.—1975
Feb., August, Nov.   —1976
Feb., May, August, Nov.—1977
Feb.   —1978

Electric Vehicle News published quarterly.
Subscription prices:
In U.S.A.—$10 for 1 year, $18 for two years, $24 for
            3 years.
Outside U.S.A.—$12 for 1 year, $22 for two years,
                $30 for 3 years.

Contact: Electric Vehicle News
          P.O. Box 533,
          Westport, Conn. 06880

"ENGINEERS IN, STYLISTS OUT"
Machine Design (Oct. 17, 1974) p. 120.

"HISTORICALLY SPEAKING, WE'VE COME A
LONG WAY"
The Battery Man (July 1975) p. 4.

"HOW MANY SPEEDS?"
Machine Design (Oct. 17, 1974) p. 139.

"MODULE-MOBILE"
Car and Driver (March 1968) p. 80.

"A NEW SPARK REVIVES ELECTRIC CAR
MAKERS"
"Business Week (Jan. 17, 1977) p. 86.

"A PIONEER STRUGGLES TO KEEP HIS PRODUCT
PLUGGED IN"
Industry Week (April 25, 1977) p. 76.

"REDDY-KILOWATT WAS MY CO-PILOT"
Car and Driver (Jan. 1978) p. 12.

"ROAD TESTING THE ELECTRICS"
Machine Design (Oct. 17, 1974) p. 19.

"SEMICONDUCTORS MEAN EXTRA RANGE"
Machine Design (Oct. 17, 1974) p. 135.

"THE WAR AGAINST THE AUTOMOBILE"
Car and Driver (Jan. 1978) p. 31.

INDEX

LIBRARY
ST. LOUIS COMMUNITY COLLEGE
AT FLORISSANT VALLEY